The New York Times

IN THE HEADLINES

School Shootings

HOW CAN WE STOP THEM?

THE NEW YORK TIMES EDITORIAL STAFF

Published in 2019 by New York Times Educational Publishing
in association with The Rosen Publishing Group, Inc.
29 East 21st Street, New York, NY 10010

First Edition

The New York Times
Alex Ward: Editorial Director, Book Development
Brenda Hutchings: Senior Photo Editor/Art Buyer
Phyllis Collazo: Photo Rights/Permissions Editor
Heidi Giovine: Administrative Manager

Rosen Publishing
Jacob R. Steinberg: Director of Content Development
Greg Tucker: Creative Director
Brian Garvey: Art Director
Greg Clinton: Editor

Cataloging-in-Publication Data
Names: New York Times Company.
Title: School shootings: how can we stop them? / edited by the
New York Times editorial staff.
Description: New York : The New York Times Educational Publishing, 2019. | Series: In the headlines | Includes glossary and index.
Identifiers: ISBN 9781642820409 (pbk.) | ISBN 9781642820393
(library bound) | ISBN 9781642820386 (ebook)
Subjects: LCSH: School shootings—United States—Juvenile
literature. | School shootings—Prevention—Juvenile literature. |
School violence—Juvenile literature. | School violence—Prevention—Juvenile literature.
Classification: LCC LB3013.3 S366 2019 | DDC 371.7'82—dc23

Manufactured in the United States of America

On the cover: Students from elementary, middle and high schools gather at Roosevelt High School in Seattle to demonstrate against gun violence March 14, 2018; Ruth Fremson/The New York Times.

Contents

CHAPTER 3

Sandy Hook: Redefining the Possibilities of Violence

CHAPTER 4

Parkland: New Tragedy, New Politics

CHATPER 5

The Future: Student Action Shaping the Debate

Introduction

GUNS HAVE A LONG political and symbolic tradition in America. Muskets defended the American colonies against unjust British rule — the birth of the United States as a country required a violent revolution. Guns also helped wrest control of the western territories from native peoples, and in the imaginary Wild West, the hero with a gun became a symbol for American (white, masculine) heroism and virtue. The gun was a symbol of law and order, of adventure, of freedom and self-sufficiency on the American frontier. The virtuous gunslinger brings order and justice to a lawless wilderness — so the story goes. According to the logic of films set in the Old West, if there is a problem, usually a gun will solve it.

Beginning in the colonial and frontier eras of American history, then, guns are at the heart of American cultural practices, especially white cultural practices. (The first black residents of the United States and its colonies were slaves, and guns were used to fight and destroy native American peoples.) Even now, guns have enormous emotional significance to many Americans. For families who hunt with rifles, the gift of a first gun can be like first steps or first words: a rite of passage, the cultivation of an ancient skill, a place in the community. Veterans of the U.S. military might see firearms as symbols of their sacrifice or of their bravery in combat.

Guns figure prominently in the politics of the United States. The Second Amendment to the Constitution declares that "a well regulated Militia, being necessary to the security of a free State, the right of the people to keep and bear Arms, shall not be infringed." This could be read in two basic ways: either that individuals should always have the right to own firearms, or that states should always have the right to

Luis Rodriguez, a student, held a memorial card for Alyssa Miriam Alhadeff, one of the victims of the shooting at Marjory Stoneman Douglas High School, outside Alyssa's funeral in North Lauderdale, Fla., on February 16, 2018.

have well-functioning defense forces (and individuals do not necessarily have the right to own whatever firearms they want). Interpretations of the Second Amendment have sparked fierce debates in the past century: should gun ownership be strictly regulated?

Advocates for unregulated gun ownership must reckon with an inconvenient truth: gun violence in America is much more common per capita than in other industrialized and wealthy nations. Gun violence increasingly plays out as a "mass shooting" — a term that generally refers to a shooting incident in which multiple (more than three) people are wounded or killed. And more tragically, these mass shootings increasingly happen at schools.

School shootings are particularly horrifying because we associate children with innocence, so an attack on a child comes to mean an attack on everyone who cherishes and protects life. Schools are supposed to be places for strengthening social foundations by giving the next generation the skills and opportunities they need to succeed. An attack on a school is thus an attack on the future of the society of which we are all members. The question that plays, as if on a loop: Why does this continue to happen, and what can we do to stop it?

School shootings have had different connotations at different moments in American history. The articles in this book reflect those changing attitudes. From Charles Whitman opening fire from a clocktower at the University of Texas at Austin in 1966 to four college students being killed by the National Guard at Kent State University in Ohio in 1970 (during protests against the Vietnam War), to mass shootings at Columbine High School in 1999 and the massacre of children at Sandy Hook Elementary School in 2012, the context and debate around guns and schools has shifted drastically over the decades.

The purpose of the collected editorials and reports on school shootings in this book is not only to provide a broad history of the events and debates, but to show how public reactions to school shootings are changing. And in the end, to pose a crucial question for Americans in the 21st century as more innocent people are threatened, injured, and killed: what is to be done?

CHAPTER 1

The University as Battleground

The University of Texas sniper in 1966 and the mass shooter at Virginia Tech in 2007 were both the murderous actions of lone individuals, bent on killing and having a troubled relationship to their educational institutions. The shooting deaths of four students at Kent State during a Vietnam War protest, however, shifted the debate about violence to the purpose of police or military force against acts of civil disobedience. The gun debate, once centered on justice and reason, has over time been complicated by self-interested political forces.

1966: 'The Time Has Come for Action'

BY DAVID W. DUNLAP | OCT. 5, 2017

AFTER A HEAVILY ARMED sniper killed more than a dozen people and wounded twice as many more by firing from a tower at the University of Texas, the president of the United States offered his thoughts and prayers to the victims' relatives, including an executive at a company the president owned.

Then, without waiting any longer, President Lyndon B. Johnson called for a response to match the deadly event.

"What happened is not without a lesson: that we must press urgently for the legislation now pending in Congress to help prevent the wrong person from obtaining firearms," Mr. Johnson said in a statement read by Bill Moyers, the White House press secretary, on

Aug. 2, 1966. That was one day after the shootings in Austin.

"The bill would not prevent all such tragedies," the statement continued. "But it would help reduce the unrestricted sale of firearms to those who cannot be trusted in their use and possession. How many lives might be saved as a consequence?

"The gun control bill has been under consideration in the Congress for many months. The time has come for action."

A day earlier, Charles Whitman, a 25-year-old student at the University of Texas, had opened fire from the U.T. Tower. Thirteen victims of the fusillade died instantly or within hours: Thomas Aquinas Ashton, 22; Robert Hamilton Boyer, 33; Thomas Frederick Eckman, 18; Martin Gabour, 16; Thomas Ray Karr, 24; Marguerite Lamport, 45; Claudia Rutt, 18; Roy Dell Schmidt, 29; Paul Bolton Sonntag, 18, whose grandfather was a news director at KTBC, owned by Mr. Johnson and his wife, Lady Bird; Officer Billy Paul Speed, 24; Edna Elizabeth Townsley, 51; Harry Walchuk, 38; and an unborn baby boy whose mother, Claire Wilson, was shot in the abdomen. Ms. Wilson survived.

Karen Griffith, 17, died of her wounds a week later. David Hubert Gunby, 23, died in 2001 of kidney disease attributable to the wound he suffered in 1966, and his death was ruled a homicide. Because Mr. Whitman had earlier killed his mother, Margaret, 43, and his wife, Kathleen, 23, the day's death toll is often placed at 17.

(Short sketches of the victims appear on the website Behind the Tower.)

"We are deeply grieved," Mr. Johnson was quoted as saying by Robert B. Semple Jr., a correspondent who was covering the president for The New York Times, alongside Charles Mohr.

Today, Mr. Semple is the associate editor of the editorial page. In between, he has been the chief White House correspondent, the deputy national editor, the London bureau chief, the foreign editor and the editor of the Op-Ed Page. He won the Pulitzer Prize in 1996 for his editorials on environmental issues.

The front page of The New York Times on August 3, 1966, two days after a mass shooting in Texas.

Immediately after the Austin killings, Mr. Semple wrote that Washington insiders were "cautious about predicting final success for a gun control bill."

"They recalled that after the assassination of President Kennedy in November 1963, there was a strong drive for passage for restrictive measures. However, the drive collapsed before the powerful opposition of the National Rifle Association and other gun clubs."

Following the assassinations of the Rev. Dr. Martin Luther King Jr. and Senator Robert F. Kennedy in 1968, Congress approved a bill regulating the interstate mail-order sales of rifles, shotguns and ammunition.

Mr. Johnson signed the legislation under protest that it did not go far enough in controlling gun ownership.

"The voices that blocked these safeguards were not the voices of an aroused nation," the president said Oct. 22, 1968. "They were the voices of a powerful gun lobby that has prevailed for the moment in an election year."

"We have been through a great deal of anguish these last few months and these last few years — too much anguish to forget so quickly," Mr. Johnson said.

It would take 16 years for the record one-day toll by a lone gunman to fall. On July 18, 1984, James Huberty killed 21 people and injured 19 at a McDonald's in San Ysidro, Calif.

The Times did not report any comment from the administration of President Ronald Reagan. His public papers show no statements on the subject in the days following.

McDonald's, however, asked broadcasters nationwide to delay its commercials for several days, out of respect.

University of Texas to Reopen Clock Tower Closed After Suicides

THE NEW YORK TIMES | NOV. 17, 1998

AFTER BEING CLOSED 23 years ago because of a series of suicides, the observation deck of the 307-foot clock tower at the University of Texas will be reopened to the public, perhaps by next spring.

The university announced last week that it would reopen the tower, which is better known as the site of a shooting that left 14 people dead and 31 wounded 32 years ago.

The tower, which is part of the university's Main Building, is one of the tallest structures in Austin. Since the tower was completed in 1937, nine people have jumped to their deaths from the observation deck, which was closed in 1975.

On Aug. 1, 1966, Charles Whitman, a student at the university, barricaded himself on the observation deck and began shooting passers-by with a rifle. At the time, the shooting was the nation's worst mass killing. It lasted 93 minutes, ending with Mr. Whitman's being killed by the police, but its after effects have spanned two generations.

Mr. Whitman, a former marine who killed his wife and his mother the night before the tower shootings, has been the subject of a movie, and many magazine and newspaper articles have been written about Mr. Whitman and the incident.

The University of Texas offers a course that examines the impact of Mr. Whitman's deeds, and bullet holes from police officers returning Mr. Whitman's fire can still be seen in the tower's facade.

"The tower is a symbol of a premier university and a very tragic event all at the same time," said Gary Lavergne, the author of a book about the shootings, "Sniper in the Tower" (UNT Press, 1997). "I can't think of another building or structure that has such a dual meaning to so many people."

Mr. Lavergne, who supports the decision to reopen the tower, said the 1966 shootings "introduced us to the modern concept of what is now called simultaneous mass murder."

The tower gives a commanding view of the campus and the city of Austin, and student groups have periodically sought to have the observation deck reopened.

Last Thursday, the university's board of regents agreed to spend about $500,000 to install iron barriers to deter suicides and to make the observation deck accessible to people with disabilities. Renovations are expected to be completed in time for spring graduation.

Under the plan, security personnel will accompany visitors to the observation deck. The university also plans to charge tower visitors an admission fee of $6 each.

In a statement, the university president, Larry Faulkner, called the tower the "most important symbol of academic aspiration and achievement in Texas." He added that it is time to "actively use this icon of higher education in positive ways."

Kara Burch, a senior, is eager to see Austin from the tower. "It's pretty exciting," Ms. Burch said. "There's been a lot of debate about the tower on campus. Before I graduate, I will be able to go up there."

Robert Heard, an Austin resident who was wounded by Mr. Whitman in 1966, agrees with the decision to reopen the tower. Mr. Heard, an Associated Press reporter when he was shot, said: "We've been long enough without the public being able to go up there. It's an idea whose time has come."

4 Kent State Students Killed by Troops

BY JOHN KIFNER | MAY 4, 1970

KENT, OHIO — Four students at Kent State University, two of them women, were shot to death this afternoon by a volley of National Guard gunfire. At least 8 other students were wounded.

The burst of gunfire came about 20 minutes after the guardsmen broke up a noon rally on the Commons, a grassy campus gathering spot, by lobbing tear gas at a crowd of about 1,000 young people.

In Washington, President Nixon deplored the deaths of the four students in the following statement:

"This should remind us all once again that when dissent turns to violence it invites tragedy. It is my hope that this tragic and unfortunate incident will strengthen the determination of all the nation's campuses, administrators, faculty and students alike to stand firmly for the right which exists in this country of peaceful dissent and just as strong against the resort to violence as a means of such expression."

In Columbus, Sylvester Del Corso, Adjutant General of the Ohio National Guard, said in a statement that the guardsmen had been forced to shoot after a sniper opened fire against the troops from a nearby rooftop and the crowd began to move to encircle the guardsmen.

Frederick P. Wenger, the Assistant Adjutant General, said the troops had opened fire after they were shot at by a sniper.

"They were understanding orders to take cover and return any fire," he said.

This reporter, who was with the group of students, did not see any indication of sniper fire, nor was the sound of any gunfire audible before the Guard volley. Students, conceding that rocks had been thrown, heatedly denied that there was any sniper.

Gov. James A. Rhodes called on J. Edgar Hoover, director of the Federal Bureau of Investigation, to aid in looking into the campus violence. A Justice Department spokesman said no decision had been made to investigate. At 2:10 this afternoon, after the shootings, the university president, Robert I. White, ordered the university closed for an indefinite time, and officials were making plans to evacuate the dormitories and bus out-of-state students to nearby cities.

Robinson Memorial Hospital identified the dead students as Allison Krause, 19 years old, of Pittsburgh; Sandra Lee Scheuer, 20, of Youngstown, Ohio, both coeds; Jeffrey Glenn Miller, 20, of 22 Diamond Drive, Plainsview, L.I., and William K. Schroeder, 19, of Lorain, Ohio.

At 10:30 P.M. the hospital said that six students had been treated for gunshot wounds. Three were reported in critical condition and three in fair condition. Two others with superficial wounds were treated and released.

Students here, angered by the expansion of the war into Cambodia, have held demonstrations for the last three nights. On Saturday night, the Army Reserve Officers Training Corps building was burned to the ground and the Guard was called in and martial law was declared.

Today's rally, called after a night in which the police and guardsmen drove students into their dormitories and made 69 arrests, began as students rang the iron Victory bell on the commons, normally used to herald football victories.

A National Guard jeep drove onto the Commons and an officer ordered the crowd to disperse. Then several canisters of tear gas were fired, and the students straggled up a hill that borders the area and retreated into buildings. A platoon of guardsmen, armed — as they have been since they arrived here with loaded M-1 rifles and gas equipment — moved across the green and over the crest of the hill, chasing the main body of protesters.

The youths split into two groups, one heading farther downhill toward a dormitory complex, the other eddying around a parking lot and girls' dormitory just below Taylor Hall, the architecture building.

The guardsmen moved into a grassy area just below the parking lot and fired several canisters of tear gas from their short, stubby launchers.

Three or four youths ran to the smoking canisters and hurled them back. Most fell far short, but one landed near the troops and a cheer went up from the crowd, which was chanting "Pigs off campus" and cursing the war.

A few youths in the front of the crowd ran into the parking lot and hurled stones or small chunks of pavement in the direction of the guardsmen. Then the troops began moving back up the hill in the direction of the college.

STUDENTS CHEER

The students in the parking lot area, numbering about 500, began to move toward the rear of the troops, cheering. Again, a few in front picked up stones from the edge of the parking lot and threw them at the guardsmen. Another group of several hundred students had gathered around the sides of Taylor Hall watching.

As the guardsmen, moving up the hill in single file, reached the crest, they suddenly turned, forming a skirmish line and opening fire.

The crackle of the rifle volley cut the suddenly still air. It appeared to go on, as a solid volley, for perhaps a full minute or a little longer.

Some of the students dived to the ground, crawling on the grass in terror. Others stood shocked or half crouched, apparently believing the troops were firing into the air. Some of the rifle barrels were pointed upward.

Near the top of the hill at the corner of Taylor Hall, a student crumpled over, spun sideways and fell to the ground, shot in the head.

When the firing stopped, a slim girl, wearing a cowboy shirt and faded jeans, was lying face down on the road at the edge of the parking lot, blood pouring out onto the macadam, about 10 feet from this reporter.

TOO SHOCKED TO REACT

The youth stood stunned, many of them clustered in small groups staring at the bodies. A young man cradled one of the bleeding forms in his arms. Several girls began to cry. But many of the students who rushed from the scene seemed almost too shocked to react. Several gathered around an abstract steel sculpture in front of the building and looked at the .30-caliber bullet hole drilled through one of the plates.

The hospital said that six young people were being treated for gunshot wounds, some in the intensive care unit. Three of the students who were killed were dead on arrival at the hospital.

One guardsman was treated and released at the hospital and another was admitted with heat prostration.

In early afternoon, students attempted to gather at various areas of the Commons but were ordered away by guardsmen and the Ohio Highway Patrol, which moved in as reinforcements.

There were no further clashes, as faculty members, graduate assistants and student leaders urged the crowd to go back to dormitories.

But a bizarre atmosphere hung over the campus as a Guard helicopter hovered overhead, grim-faced officers maneuvered their men to safeguard the normally pastoral campus and students, dazed, fearful and angry, struggled to comprehend what had happened and to find something to do about it.

Students carrying suitcases and duffel bags began leaving the campus this afternoon. Early tonight the entire campus was sealed off and a court injunction was issued ordering all students to leave.

A 5 P.M. curfew was declared in Kent, and road blocks were set up around the town to prevent anyone from entering. A state of emergency was also declared in the nearby towns of Stow and Ravenna.

Virginia Tech Shooting Leaves 33 Dead

BY CHRISTINE HAUSER AND ANAHAD O'CONNOR | APRIL 16, 2007

THIRTY-THREE PEOPLE were killed Monday on the campus of Virginia Tech in what appears to be the deadliest shooting rampage in American history, according to federal law enforcement officials. Many of the victims were students shot in a dorm and a classroom building.

"Today, the university was struck with a tragedy that we consider of monumental proportions," said the university's president, Charles Steger. The campus police chief said this evening that 15 people were wounded by the gunman, although there were other reports of higher numbers of injuries.

Witnesses described scenes of mass chaos and unimaginable horror as some students were lined up against a wall and shot. Others

Virginia Tech students prayed in a church near the university after a shooting rampage.

jumped out of windows to escape, or crouched on floors to take cover.

The killings occurred in two separate attacks on the campus in Blacksburg, Va. The first took place around 7:15 a.m., when two people were shot and killed at a dormitory. More than two and a half hours later, 31 others, including the gunman, were shot and killed across campus in a classroom building, where some of the doors had been chained. Victims were found in different locations around the building.

The first attack started as students were getting ready for classes or were on their way there. The university did not evacuate the campus or notify students of that attack until several hours later.

As the rampage unfolded, details emerged from witnesses describing a gunman going room to room in a dormitory, Ambler Johnston Hall, and of gunfire later at Norris Hall, a science and engineering classroom building. When it was over, even sidewalks were stained with blood. Among those dead was the gunman, whose body was found along with victims in Norris Hall.

"Norris Hall is a tragic and sorrowful crime scene," said the campus police chief at Virginia Tech, Wendell Flinchum.

Chief Flinchum said the gunman took his own life. He said at a televised news briefing Monday evening that the police had a preliminary identification of the suspected gunman but were not yet ready to release it. He said the gunman was not a student.

According to a federal law enforcement official, the gunman did not have identification and could not be easily identified visually because of the severity of an apparently self-inflicted wound to the head. He said investigators were trying to trace purchase records for two handguns found near the body.

At televised news conferences Monday afternoon and Monday evening, Chief Flinchum and Mr. Steger tried to explain why authorities did not act to secure the rest of the campus immediately after the first shooting.

Chief Flinchum said that initially officials thought that the shooting was "domestic," suggesting that it was between individuals who knew each other, and isolated to the dormitory. He said the campus was not shut down after the first shooting because authorities thought that the attacker may have left the campus, or even the state.

"We knew we had two people shot," he said. "We secured the building. We secured the crime scene." He later added: "We acted on the best information we had at the time."

Chief Flinchum said officers initially began investigating a "person of interest" as a result of the dormitory shootings. The person, a man, was described as a friend of one of the dorm victims, but Chief Flinchum said the police had not detained him.

At 9:45, the police got another 911 call about shootings at Norris Hall, just as university officials were meeting to discuss the first shootings. "We were actually having a meeting about the earlier shootings when we learned that another shooting was under way," Mr. Steger told reporters Monday night. By the time officers arrived, the shooting had stopped and the gunman had killed himself, the chief said.

The police appeared to believe that the two shootings were related, but said they could not confirm that until they had the results of a ballistics analysis.

A parent of one student, Elaine Goss, said her son Alec Calhoun, a junior engineering major, jumped out a second-story window in Norris Hall when the gunman entered his classroom.

She said that she first spoke to her son, "I couldn't understand him; it was like gibberish."

"It took a while to figure out shootings, lots of shootings, and that his whole class had jumped out the window," she said.

Ms. Goss said her son hurt his back in the jump and went to a hospital.

Another student, Jessica Paulson, said she was on the fourth floor at Ambler Johnston Hall when the shootings occurred on the opposite side of the floor.

"You could hear two shots," one followed shortly by a second, recounted Ms. Paulson, who was preparing to go to an early class.

Neither she nor most of the other students nearby understood what had happened until several hours later.

At least 17 Virginia Tech students were being treated for gunshot wounds and other injuries at Montgomery Regional Hospital, and four of them were in surgery, according to a hospital spokesman. At Lewis-Gale Medical Center in Salem, Va., four students and a staff member were treated for injuries. Two were in stable condition, and the conditions of the other three were described as "undetermined."

Officials said there may have been more injured and taken to other medical facilities.

The university has more than 25,000 full-time students on a campus that is spread over 2,600 acres.

The atmosphere on the Virginia Tech campus was desolate and preternaturally quiet by Monday afternoon. Students gathered in small groups, some crying, some talking quietly and others consoling each other.

Some students complained that they had not been notified of the first shooting on campus for more than two hours.

Kirsten Bernhards, 18, said she and many other students had no idea that a shooting had occurred when she left her dorm room in O'Shaughnessy Hall shortly before 10 a.m., more than two hours after the first shootings.

"I was leaving for my 10:10 film class," she said. "I had just locked the door and my neighbor said, 'Did you check your e-mail?' "

The university had, a few minutes earlier, sent out a bulletin warning students about an apparent gunman. But few students seemed to have any sense of urgency.

Ms. Bernhards said she walked toward her class, preoccupied with an upcoming exam and listening to music on her iPod. On the way, she said, she heard some loud cracks, and only later concluded they had been gunshots from the second round of shootings.

But even at that point, many students were walking around the campus with little if any sense of alarm.

It was only when Ms. Bernhards got close to Norris Hall, the second of two buildings where the shootings took place, that she realized that something had gone wrong.

"I looked up and I saw at least 10 guards with assault rifles aiming at the main entrance of Norris," she recalled.

Up until Monday, the deadliest campus shooting in United States history was in 1966 at the University of Texas, where Charles Whitman climbed to the 28th-floor observation deck of a clock tower and opened fire, killing 16 people before he was gunned down by the police. In the Columbine High attack in Colorado in 1999, two teenagers killed 12 fellow students and a teacher before killing themselves.

While few confirmed details about the gunman and the motive were clear, students told reporters at WTKR, a local television station, that the gunman had been looking for his girlfriend, and at one of the locations he lined up some students and shot them all, according to Mike Mather, a reporter for the station.

President Bush offered condolences this afternoon to relatives of the victims, and said federal investigators would help the Virginia authorities in any way possible. "We hold the victims in our hearts; we lift them up in our prayers," Mr. Bush said at the White House.

President Bush was "horrified" at the news of the shooting, said Dana Perino, a White House spokeswoman, earlier in the day.

One student captured partial images, broadcast on CNN, using his cellphone video camera. They showed grainy dark-clad figures on the street outside campus buildings. Popping sounds from the gunfire were audible.

"This place is in a state of panic," said a student who was interviewed on CNN, Shaver Deyerle. "Nobody knew what was going on at first."

He said the shootings reminded him of the Columbine High School killings.

The shootings at Virginia Tech come in the same week, eight years ago, as the shooting at Columbine on April 20, 1999.

The police were slowly evacuating students from campus buildings and all classes were canceled.

Families were told to reunite with students at the Inn at Virginia Tech, a facility of conference space and hotel rooms. University employees were told to assemble on Tuesday at the Cassell Coliseum to start to deal with the tragedy, a campus statement said.

Images on CNN showed the police with assault rifles swarming several buildings, sirens blaring in the background and a voice over a loudspeaker warning people across the campus to take cover in buildings and stay away from windows. Many students could be seen crouching on floors in classrooms and dormitories.

The police evacuated some students and faculty members, many of them to local hotels, and witnesses said some students were seen scrambling out of windows to get to safety. A Montgomery County school official said that all schools throughout the county were being shut down.

The shooting was the second in the past year that forced officials to lock down the campus. In August of 2006, an escaped jail inmate shot and killed a deputy sheriff and an unarmed security guard at a nearby hospital before the police caught him in the woods near the university.

The capture ended a manhunt that led to the cancellation of the first day of classes at Virginia Tech and shut down most businesses and municipal buildings in Blacksburg. The shooting suspect, William Morva, is facing capital murder charges.

At Virginia Tech, Remembering While Moving On

BY SHAILA DEWAN AND ARIEL SABAR | AUG. 20, 2007

BLACKSBURG, VA. — By move-in day this weekend, the freshman class at Virginia Tech already knew a few of the ropes. Packed into the bleachers of Cassell Coliseum in their orange and maroon T-shirts on Saturday night, they began to jump up and down in unison at the opening chords of "Enter Sandman," the Metallica anthem. At the sound of "Hokie Hokie Hokie, Hi!" they joined in with the 111-year-old nonsense cheer that gave the university mascot its name.

But Seth Greenberg, the men's basketball coach, had something more to tell them.

"After the tragedy of 4/16 last year, you saw the best of the Virginia Tech students," he said, pacing the floor of the basketball court. "Their ownership, their passion, their commitment to their university was second to none. They love this school. They believe in this school. And that's the pride that you have to take each and every day as you walk across this campus."

As students return to classes here Monday, just four months after the country's deadliest shooting rampage took 33 lives and devastated the campus, Virginia Tech is walking a fine line between remembering and moving on. It must welcome eager freshmen while embracing faculty members and students who are grieving and, in some cases, still recovering from physical injuries.

Before freshman orientation in July, the student center was stripped of the banners, gifts and cards that poured in after the shooting. But on Sunday afternoon, the central event was the dedication of a memorial to the victims in the symbolic heart of the campus, the Drillfield.

T-shirts proclaiming "We are Virginia Tech," the rallying cry taken from the poem written by Nikki Giovanni after the shooting, are everywhere on campus. But in an effort to avoid being defined solely by

CASEY TEMPLETON FOR THE NEW YORK TIMES

Mariella Lurch grieved at the stone honoring her brother, Daniel Perez Cueva, 21, at the dedication of the memorial Sunday.

tragedy, the university has not permitted merchandise that juxtapose the date April 16 with the university's name or trademarks.

Like Coach Greenberg, many officials have tried to emphasize the grace of the campus response, an approach that resonates both with those who lived through the crisis and those who watched it on television. Although the shooting occurred two weeks before tuition deposits were due, Virginia Tech saw no decline in the percentage of students accepting its admission offers. And of the 25 students injured in the shooting, 19 will be returning to classes this fall, said Mark Owczarski, a university spokesman.

Kim Bereznak, a freshman, had already decided to accept Virginia Tech's offer before the shooting, but what she saw afterward reinforced her decision. "It made me proud, personally, just how strong everyone was," she said. "They could have turned their back on their school, but they didn't."

Returning students voiced some apprehension, but said they were more relieved to end a summer of intrusive questions from people back home.

"It's to the point where you just want to go be in Blacksburg, be with the Hokies, be with your family," said Robert Bowman, a senior and the president of the Hokie Ambassadors, who lead campus tours. Still, he added, there is a craving for normalcy. "By tomorrow there will be more students complaining about their chemistry professor than talking about April 16. We will be back."

If questions from outsiders can be jarring, the rampage is still a frequent topic of conversation among friends, said Grant Duncan, a sophomore. "It's good to continue to talk about it," he said. "It definitely just helps the healing process."

Derek O'Dell, 20, who was shot in the arm as he tried to bar the student gunman, Seung-Hui Cho, from his classroom, said he was thrilled to be back despite having anxiety attacks. "I don't really know how

CASEY TEMPLETON FOR THE NEW YORK TIMES

Jeff Fleming, a Virginia Tech alumnus, looked through merchandise showing school spirit at the campus bookstore.

well I'll be able to concentrate, but I definitely want to be back here," he said. "The Hokie Nation, being back here now, it's even more of a sense of belonging."

In a letter about the news media presence expected on campus this week, Lawrence G. Hincker, the vice president for university relations, told students to feel free to decline any interview. "Should you engage a reporter," he wrote, "take advantage of the opportunity to share some Hokie spirit. The world mourned with us and maintains an interest in the collective health of our extended university community."

Rick Sparks Jr., the director of orientation, said that when the student orientation leaders arrived, he was prepared to spend hours talking through the trauma. But that was not necessary. "They were anxious about getting questions," he said, "but other than that they were ready to do their jobs."

The banners and other gifts were removed from the student center, he said, because they might have overwhelmed newcomers. Freshmen and their parents were offered a session where the campus police answered questions about the shooting and security, but very few attended, Mr. Sparks said.

New security measures include an emergency text-messaging system for student cellphones and 24-hour locks at residence halls. New locks have also been installed on classroom doors, and door handles on classroom buildings will be harder to chain shut, as Mr. Cho did before the shooting.

Susanna Rinehart, a theater professor, said she would wait to see her students' mood before deciding how to discuss the shooting.

"It's so hard to say what it feels like to be a faculty member here right now," said Ms. Rinehart, whose first class on Monday, an arts survey, will have more than 500 students from all majors. "We all, I think, just feel this sort of inner shakiness, this sort of not knowing what it's going to feel like, and knowing that we can't know."

How Many More Warnings?

OPINION | BY THE NEW YORK TIMES | FEB. 11, 2008

EVEN WITH FAMILIES victimized in the Virginia Tech massacre looking on, lawmakers in Virginia lined up like clay pigeons for the gun
lobby last month to block legislation that would have closed the state's
notorious gun-show loophole. That means that anyone — ex-felons
and deranged citizens included — can continue to buy firearms at
laissez-faire "sportsmen" shows.

The life-saving bill was supported by frontline police organizations,
Gov. Tim Kaine and a majority of Virginians, still mourning the deadliest campus shooting in American history. That didn't stop opponents
from claiming that the problem had already been solved. It hasn't.

In the wake of the massacre, Congress was finally shamed into
passing legislation intended to improve national record-keeping and
make it harder for people with a criminal history or a history of dangerous mental illness — like the Virginia Tech gunman — to purchase
firearms from licensed gun dealers. Threat closed? No.

The lethal truth is that even if the troubled student had been denied
by licensed dealers, he could have easily turned to the many unlicensed
peddlers at weekend open-air shows, where gun worship trumps public
safety, to buy his high-tech arsenal and ammunition. In one of America's many earlier warnings, the killers responsible for the Columbine
High School massacre did their shopping at Colorado gun shows.

The Virginia Legislature's failure mocks all of the high-minded
promises of closure uttered in the blood and grief after the tragedy. It
again underlines the need for federal legislation to close gun-show loopholes. A bipartisan bill is already awaiting action, but the gun lobby
never rests. The presidential candidates should show that they have
more grit than Virginia's lawmakers and demand an end to unlicensed
gun shows, and demand that Congress show courage and sense of
its own.

When the Group Is Wise

BY BENEDICT CAREY | APRIL 22, 2007

SEUNG-HUI CHO seemed indifferent to every small act of human kindness, any effort to connect.

According to classmates of Mr. Cho, the Virginia Tech killer, one student made several attempts to speak to him, even after reading his frightening writings. Mr. Cho's suitemates, and some teachers, too, made an effort to engage him. And there were undoubtedly others. Maybe they signaled their openness with a slight nod, a friendly widening of the eyes.

Those acts of genuine decency failed to prevent Mr. Cho's rampage on Monday. But the tragedy in Blacksburg, Va., illustrates how human social groups, whether in classrooms, boardrooms or dormitories, are in fact exquisitely sensitive to a threat in their midst, and act in ways both conscious and unconscious to test how dangerous it is. Take a step back, and the peer group can be seen as a single organism that recoils from a threat, then sends out feelers, in the form of overtures from its members, to gauge whether danger is imminent or might be reduced.

The Blacksburg case suggests just how this process typically works, and highlights its strengths as well as its limits in preventing a crisis.

After this shooting (and most school and workplace rampages, big and small), forensic experts quickly and properly cautioned that no profile of a rampage killer exists. Most predatory killers score very highly on the most rigorously tested measure to predict violence, the so-called psychopathy checklist; but many who do not commit crimes also score high.

Yet out in the world, no one uses questionnaires or diagnostic manuals to check out a stranger or an acquaintance. People read the other person's body language, tone of voice; they read between the lines of what is said. They absorb most of this information instantly, unconsciously, and often accurately, studies suggest. And they sometimes get the creeps — for reasons they might not be able to explain right away.

The evidence that this happened over the months and years before the shooting in Blacksburg is now abundant. After hearing Mr. Cho read one of his sinister poems in a creative-writing class, dozens of his classmates did not show up the next time the class met, so as to avoid the young man, according to the teacher. This is what most human social groups do, when they collectively register a threat: they move away, socially and often literally.

The thousands of years that early humans lived in small, fragile kin groups helped shape their instinct for social distancing, anthropologists say. A person who steals, who lies or who incites fights is a direct threat not only to those lured into confrontations but also to the coherence and ultimate survival of the group itself.

"Social stigma is rooted in part in a concern for social predictability," said Robert Kurzban, a psychologist at the University of Pennsylvania. "One thing that's crucial in groups, particularly small groups, is cooperation, and if someone is unpredictable, they don't cooperate or coordinate well and represent a group threat. So people look out for such individuals."

To guard against a real threat, this instinct is naturally conservative. It flags as potentially threatening many people who aren't, as millions of people living with mental illness have experienced firsthand.

In some ancient societies and religious communities, the rules that guided how to manage a person thought to be dangerous were very explicit, said David Sloan Wilson, an evolutionary biologist at the State University of New York at Binghamton and the author of "Evolution for Everyone." Bad gossip, followed by a rebuke, then ostracism. Each stage sets in motion more isolation. This escalating discipline protects the community but is also intended to bring about a change of heart in the outcast.

Finally, if such a change isn't forthcoming, there is expulsion. "For some nomadic cultures, it was as simple as saying, 'O.K., you go this way, we're going that way,' " Dr. Wilson said.

Modern societies are — blessedly, for most people — far more tolerant. Their justice systems are less likely to be swayed by hearsay, or claims of possession and superstition. People perceived as threatening have some civil rights, and as the Virginia Tech case showed, the authorities are limited in what they can do if a person of interest hasn't actually made threats or attacks.

Still, the peer group is tracking the person carefully and, deliberately or not, doing its own tests for a threat.

For some 20 years, Lawrence Palinkas, a professor of social work at the University of Southern California, has studied the social networks that form like crystals among work teams who spend the winter together in scientific missions in Antarctica. The groups, which range in size from a dozen people to nearly 200, very often have at least one outcast. That person may be simply unlucky, picked on by influential people central to the group. But often the person helps define the identities of those who make up the group's core.

"It's a stable situation, because in a way that isolated person helps define a group; people look at him and can say, 'I'm not like him, someone who doesn't fit in,' " Dr. Palinkas said.

It often happens, Dr. Palinkas has found, that another group member makes an investment and helps reel the outcast back in. But this is much more likely to succeed when the main group is a cohesive one, like a team or work crew with a tightly bound inner core, Dr. Palinkas said. "If it's a group that is split into factions, diffuse, not well integrated, then it is very hard to integrate the isolates," he said.

Large college campuses tend to be tolerant, fluid, self-enclosed societies, where almost anyone can find a niche. The peer group around Mr. Cho, even as he avoided direct eye contact, seemed to be extending a tentacle now and then, to see if the young man was ready to find his own place. The student who tried to talk to Mr. Cho in English class, Ross Alameddine, made several attempts.

Mr. Cho ignored every one, and many more from others who were less patient.

Debate will undoubtedly continue about what could have, or should have, been done by university officials, campus police officers or the Virginia mental health system. Teachers will have their say, as will administrators.

But it is clear from interviews that many of Mr. Cho's peers knew in their guts the danger the young man presented. They sent up alarms, even while watching him. They kept their distance, as a natural protective instinct.

And through the spirit of people like Mr. Alameddine, who would become one of the random shooting victims, they continued to send out feelers: small human invitations that, in the shadow of what was to come, now look very large indeed.

CHAPTER 2

Columbine: The Modern School Shooting Era

The assault weapons, explosives and military-style coordination two high school students used to attack peers and teachers at Columbine High School in Littleton, Colorado, in 1999 set the stage for the modern era of school shootings in America. Mass shooters since then have cited the Columbine gunmen as inspiration for their own attacks. The national discussion changed to focus on mental health services that might have detected or prevented the attacks, how easily the gunmen gained access to military-grade weaponry, the impact of trauma on communities and the connections between media, fame and mass murder.

Terror In Littleton: 2 Students In Colorado School Said To Gun Down As Many As 23 And Kill Themselves In A Siege

BY JAMES BROOKE | APRIL 21, 1999

IN THE DEADLIEST school massacre in the nation's history, two young men stormed into a suburban high school here at lunch time today with guns and explosives, killing as many as 23 students and teachers and wounding at least 20 in a five-hour siege, the authorities said.

The two students who are believed to have been the gunmen, Eric

Harris and Dylan Klebold, who were students at Columbine High School, were found dead of self-inflicted gunshot wounds in the library, said Steve Davis, the spokesman for the Jefferson County Sheriff's Department.

Beginning about 11:30 A.M., the gunmen, wearing ski masks, stalked through the school as they fired semiautomatic weapons at students and teachers and tossed explosives, with one student being hit nine times in the chest by shrapnel, the authorities said. Gunshots continued to ring out at the school for hours. One bomb exploded in the library, officials said, and one in a car outside. Two more cars were rigged with bombs.

About 3 P.M., hundreds of police officers evacuated the building and searched for the gunmen. Their bodies and those of several of their victims appeared to have been wired with explosives.

Sheriff John Stone said, "It appears to be a suicide mission."

Mr. Davis said that as many as 25 people were dead, "a mixture of students and faculty." He said that most of the bodies were found in the school's entrance, the library and the commons cafeteria. No precise death toll was available.

Kaleb Newberry, 16, said: "I was in class and one teacher came in and basically told us to run for our lives, I saw a girl maybe five paces behind me fall. She was shot in the leg, but a teacher helped her."

Students said the gunmen were part of a group of misfits who called themselves the trench coat mafia, which expressed disdain for racial minorities and athletes. Members of the group found their way out of anonymity at the school by banding together, dressing in dark gothic-style clothing including long black coats. They became easy to notice among the 1,870 students at the school, since every day, regardless of the weather, they wore their coats.

Today the gunmen appeared to aim at minority members and athletes at the 1,800-student school, as well as peers who had poked fun at the group in the past.

School officials had had no reports of trouble from the suspects, Mr. Davis said.

Some victims were forced to wait inside the school for rescue. By early evening, bodies had not been removed because of the crime scene investigation and the possible presence of explosives, a spokesman for the Jefferson County Sheriff's Department said.

Mr. Davis said at a news conference tonight that two other students at the school, thought to be friends of the gunmen, were in custody for questioning in connection with the shooting.

"You can't really go in and do this kind of damage without a lot of preparation." Mr. Davis said, "without a lot of ammunition and apparently some type of bombs."

Fourteen-year-old Katie Corona, said she was trapped in a classroom with her teacher and about 30 classmates for hours.

"I thought I was going to die," she said. "I really didn't think I was going to make it. We would hear shots, then we heard crying. We had no clue what was going on."

"Everyone around me got shot and I begged him for 10 minutes not to shoot me," one young woman, who was not identified, said tonight in an interview broadcast on the Cable News Network. "And he just put the gun in my face and started laughing and saying it was all because people were mean to him last year."

Another student, who said she heard more gunshots while hiding in the closet with a teacher and some friends, said she kept thinking to herself, "This can't be happening to our school."

"You should be safe at school," added a second young woman, who also was not identified. "This should be a safe place."

The families of those killed were being notified tonight at Leawood Elementary School, where students and parents had gathered.

The mass shooting was the first at an American school during this academic year, but revived memories of similar tragedies that struck six different communities last year and set off national alarms about teen-age violence. Four girls and a teacher were shot to death and 10 people were wounded during a false fire alarm at a middle school in Jonesboro, Ark., last March.

President Clinton immediately dispatched a crisis-response team to aid the school community and the victim's families.

"We don't know yet all the how's or why's of this tragedy; perhaps we will never fully understand it," the President said in a nationally televised news conference just before 8 P.M. "St. Paul reminds us that we all see things in life darkly, that we only partly understand what is happening."

He added, "We do know that we must do more to reach out to our children and teach them to express their anger and to resolve their conflicts with words, not weapons."

A sunny spring day turned into a bloody nightmare for this suburb of 35,000 people southwest of Denver, as ambulances ferried the injured from the high school, past tennis courts, a baseball diamond and a packed student parking lot.

"I hope we can all pull together, because we will need all our strengths," Jane Hammond, Jefferson County superintendent of schools, said tonight. The blood banks in the Denver area have been overwhelmend with calls from donors. Tonight at least three church vigils for the dead and injured.

Just before 8 P.M., Lisa Appleton, 16, a sophomore, waited in front of the Leawood school for news of her best friend, Julie Toms, who had been missing since students began leaving the school.

"I can't even feel it," she said. "There's no way to know whether she's dead or alive."

About 3 P.M., SWAT teams police officers used a fire truck and an armored car to get close to the building, dozens of students raced out of the two-story building, some slipping in the mud, others holding up their hands in the air or behind their heads. Police said they feared that the gunmen would try to escape by mingling with the trapped students.

One student, bloodied from an injury, broke out a second-story window, and climbed down into the hands of the police.

As police officers established a wide perimeter around the beige school, students and school workers gathered on nearby tree-lined streets and told of the chaos and horror inside the building.

As fire alarms rang in the halls, students who had seen the gunmen trampled each other to get out of the building, running through one exit where three bodies lay on a staircase.

Trapped inside, others took refuge in classrooms, bathrooms and a choir room, frantically barricading doors with desks and file cabinets.

One cafeteria worker who barricaded herself in a woman's bathroom said, "We could hear them blowing the heck out of the place."

A student, Jonathan Ladd, said, "I heard gunshots going off, bullets ricocheting off lockers."

The trench coat mafia is a small band of about a dozen juniors and seniors at Columbine who are easily recognized yet little feared, according to people who live in the neighborhood near the school. Regardless of the weather, they favor long black coats and the Gothic look popularized by the rock singer Marilyn Manson, neighbors said. Some even wear white pancake makeup and dark eyeliner, one student said.

"It was that devilish, half-dead, half-alive look," said Bret, a 16-year-old sophomore who spoke on the condition only his first name be used.

The group often gathered in the cafeteria after school. Chris McCaffrey, manager of Angie's Restaurant a few blocks from Columbine, said that residents had known about the group for about five years, and that no one considered it a threat.

"Mostly it was just kids who nobody wanted to have anything to do with," Mr. McCaffrey said. "They weren't particularly feared. They were just a bunch of punks who kind of hang around the school."

Students said the group was mostly boys, but that some girls appeared to be closely associated with it. One student described the group as "nerds, geeks and dweebs trying to find someplace to fit in."

Bret suggested the mafia might have targeted athletes out of resentment for their own lack of popularity and success at school.

The students "weren't really accepted as younger kids and as they got older they were accepted by this group," Bret said. "They got their fair share of being picked on. I could understand that they might have targeted some of the more popular kids."

David Mesch, another student, who was searching for his mother who works for the school, said, "They were wearing masks; they were members of the trench coat mafia."

President Clinton said tonight that he was "profoundly shocked and saddened by the tragedy today in Littleton."

In an age when cellular telephones are increasingly common among high school students, several trapped students called television stations when they could not get through on 911 lines.

"I hear a couple of gunshots, people running up and down," a student said in a frightened whisper to KUSA-TV, a Denver television station. Identifying himself only as James, he added, "There are a bunch of kids downstairs, I can hear them crying."

Aware that the gunmen might be watching on a classroom television set, he said, "I am staying upstairs," and then hung up.

In a state with a relatively low crime rate, the siege after the shootings was broadcast live by Denver television stations, without commercial breaks all afternoon. Broadcast and cable networks turned to local affiliates for help with their coverage.

"This is a cultural virus," Gov. Bill Owens of Colorado said before hurrying to the scene. Noting that he felt particularly affected by the tragedy because his 16-year-old daughter goes to a suburban Denver high school, he said, "We have to ask ourselves what kind of children we are raising."

At the White House, the President said the nation should focus on praying for the victims' families and others at the school. He said that Attorney General Janet Reno was closely monitoring the situation, and that he had spoken this afternoon with Governor Owens and Patricia Holloway, the county commissioner, whose comments he shared with the nation.

In midafternoon, police officers briefly detained three young white men who wore camouflaged pants and black jackets, next to the high school. After they were released, the men said they knew the gunmen inside the high school. Emblazoned on the back of one man's jacket were the words, "Ban Religion" and a red-painted stop sign printed over a cross.

"Blood was going all over," a shaken girl said, as she was comforted by her father. Those here were reminded of other school shooting incidents.

Bob Sapin, a student, told a television station minutes after watching the shootings, "I just can't believe it is happening at my school."

In the New West, Violence Is Real

BY PATRICIA NELSON LIMERICK | APRIL 24, 1999

FIVE YEARS AGO, I spent a summer researching the wars between the United States and various Indian peoples. Most of that summer I was an insomniac, waking every night to thoughts of bleeding bodies, fractured bones and internal organs exposed to the air. Here is one of a thousand stories that made each night too long.

During the Modoc War in the Pacific Northwest in 1873, Maurice Fitzgerald, a white trooper in the United States Army wrote an account of his experiences. At one point he had seen a captive Indian woman "begging piteously for her life." " 'Me no hurt no one, me no fight,' she whined," Fitzgerald wrote.

An officer, hearing her cries, was not moved. Fitzgerald recorded his reaction. " 'Is there anyone here who will put that old hag out of the way?' A Pennsylvania Dutchman stepped forward and said, 'I'll fix her, Lieutenant.' He put the muzzle of his carbine to her head and blew it to pieces," Fitzgerald wrote.

The memory of violence comes in different forms. In one form, the images of flesh being torn and of a life ending block the approach of all other thoughts and feelings. In another, the memory comes and goes, held off by the mind till it comes back with tidal force in unexpected surges.

There is yet another kind of memory that wraps violence in justification and righteousness. While individual misfortune may have occurred, this form of memory insists, it advanced a greater cause — for instance, gaining control of the American continent.

Most peculiar of all is the kind of memory that has taken possession of the history of violence that characterized so much of what happened in the American West in the 19th century. The Alamo, the Little Big Horn, Wounded Knee have not been forgotten. They are familiar names, imbedded deep in the national memory. They seldom endure as examples of brutality and misery but rather as instances of romance and adventure.

We tend to associate the deadening of feeling and the anesthetizing of historical memory with movies, television and video games. But in the case of the American West, the process dates back much further, to the dime novels and children's games invented more than a century ago. In this way, some of the most gruesome events in our past have become episodes in the historical theme park known as the Wild West.

Thus, we hear of outlaws and their "gunplay." The tales of the James Boys, Wyatt Earp, Wild Bill Hickok and the Gunfight at the O.K. Corral are rendered as colorful, romantic yarns, bloodless and "lite," even as the mess bullets made of human bodies is all but erased from memory.

Does the trivializing of the violence of the Old West cause violence in the New West? Probably not, but I think it has contributed to a much broader contemporary shortfall in compassion, empathy and the capacity to respond seriously to the sufferings of others.

Now there are signs that the anesthetic may be wearing off. After the killings in Littleton, Colo., no one would think of using adjectives like "adventurous" to describe the latest violent chapter in the American West. No sane person is denying the impact of bullets on human flesh.

In this way, then, if in no other, the reaction to the terrible events in Littleton suggests that contemporary society is not as hopeless as it is made out to be.

The Columbine Killers

OPINION | BY DAVID BROOKS | APRIL 24, 2004

FIVE YEARS AGO, Eric Harris and Dylan Klebold shot up Columbine High School. Now it's clear that much of what we thought about that horror was wrong.

In the weeks following the killings, commentators and psychologists filled the air with theories about what on earth could have caused those teenagers to lash out as they did. The main one was that Harris and Klebold were the victims of brutal high school bullies. They were social outcasts, persecuted by the jocks and the popular kids. But there were other theories afloat: they'd fallen in with a sick Goth subculture; they were neglected by their families; they were influenced by violent video games; they were misfits who could find no place in a conformist town.

All these theories had one theme in common: that the perpetrators were actually victims. They had been so oppressed and distorted by society that they struck back in this venomous way. In retrospect, it's striking how avidly we clung to this perpetrator-as-victim narrative. It's striking how quickly we took the massacre as proof that there must be something rotten at Columbine High School.

As we've learned more about Harris and Klebold, most of these misconceptions have been exposed. The killers were not outcasts. They did not focus their fire on jocks or Christians or minorities. They were not really members of a "Trenchcoat Mafia."

This week, in a superb piece in Slate magazine, Dave Cullen reveals the conclusions of the lead F.B.I. investigator, Dwayne Fuselier, as well as of the Michigan State psychiatrist Frank Ochberg and others who studied the Columbine shootings.

Harris and Klebold "laughed at petty school shooters," Cullen reports. They sought murder on a grander scale. They planned first to set off bombs in the school cafeteria to kill perhaps 600. Then they would shoot the survivors as they fled. Then their cars, laden with still more bombs, would explode amid the rescue workers and parents rushing to the school. It all might have come off if they had not miswired the timers on the propane bombs in the cafeteria.

What motivated them? Here, Cullen says, it is necessary to distinguish Klebold from Harris. Klebold was a depressed and troubled kid who could have been saved. Harris was an icy killer. He once thought about hijacking a plane and flying it into Manhattan.

Harris wasn't bullied by jocks. He was disgusted by the inferior breed of humanity he saw around him. He didn't suffer from a lack of self-esteem. He had way too much self-esteem.

It's clear from excerpts of Harris's journals that he saw himself as a sort of Nietzschean Superman — someone so far above the herd of ant-like mortals he does not even have to consider their feelings. He rises above good and evil, above the contemptible slave morality of normal people. He can realize his true, heroic self, and establish his eternal glory, only through some gigantic act of will.

"Harris was not a wayward boy who could have been rescued," Cullen writes. Harris, the F.B.I. experts believe, "was irretrievable."

Now, in 2004, we have more experience with suicidal murderers. Yet it is striking how resilient this perpetrator-as-victim narrative remains. We still sometimes assume that the people who flew planes into buildings — and those who blew up synagogues in Turkey, trains in Spain, discos in Tel Aviv and schoolchildren this week in Basra — are driven by feelings of weakness, resentment and inferiority. We cling to the egotistical notion that it is our economic and political dominance that drives terrorists insane.

But it could be that whatever causes they support or ideologies they subscribe to, the one thing that the killers have in common is a feeling of immense superiority. It could be that they want to exterminate us because they regard us as spiritually deformed and unfit to live, at least in their world. After all, it is hard to pull up to a curb, look a group of people in the eye and know that in a few seconds you will shred them to pieces unless you regard other people's deaths as trivialities.

If today's suicide bombers are victims of oppression, then the solution is to lessen our dominance, and so assuage their resentments. But if they are vicious people driven by an insatiable urge to dominate, then our only option is to fight them to the death.

We had better figure out who these bombers really are. After Columbine, we got it wrong.

When Columbine Is Invoked, Fears Tend to Overshadow Facts

BY CLYDE HABERMAN | SEPT. 27, 2015

IT TAKES NEITHER a clairvoyant nor a morbid personality to sense that, in time, the nightmare will return. We have already seen it often enough: Someone goes berserk and shoots up a school — typically a young man who turns a gun on himself after taking children's lives, shattering families and leaving a tormented country to ponder how things went terribly wrong. Once again.

School shootings have become so much a part of the American experience that many people assume the atrocities are happening ever more frequently. But are they? The question is not simple, and evidence can be murky, if only because studies using differing methodologies arrive at varying conclusions. In search of answers, Retro Report, a series of video documentaries exploring major news stories of the past and their lasting impact, examines one of the worst shootings, a moment in 1999 so searing that it is still instantly evoked with a single word: Columbine.

The massacre of 12 students and a teacher at Columbine High School, outside Denver, was not the first mass killing at a school. By then, dots on the map like Jonesboro, Ark., and West Paducah, Ky., had been pushed into the national spotlight because of such shootings.

Columbine, however, was different. Not only was it the most lethal attack on an American high school, but it also unfolded on television in real time, with teenagers cowering under desks and using mobile phones to report what they had seen or heard. It was "the first major hostage standoff of the cellphone age," Dave Cullen wrote in "Columbine," his well-received 2009 book about the ordeal. The police, he said, "had never seen anything like it."

Columbine became a model for subsequent shootings. In writings they left behind, the young men who killed dozens at Virginia Tech in

2007 and in Newtown, Conn., in 2012 spoke of being inspired by Columbine. Yet as Mr. Cullen makes clear, and as the Retro Report video demonstrates, much of what the public came to believe about Columbine was flat-out wrong. Myths took root from the start, nurtured by frightened and confused students and amplified by news outlets running hard with rumor and conjecture.

The story line that unspooled ran like this: The student killers, Eric Harris and Dylan Klebold, belonged to a group at the school called the Trench Coat Mafia, said to be goth outcasts. The pair had been subjected repeatedly to bullying, especially by self-impressed jocks. And so this was a mission of revenge. The two young men went hunting for athletes, nonwhites and those professing a love of God, singling them out as targets before holing up in the school library and turning their guns on themselves.

Almost none of this proved to be true. In fact, as Mr. Cullen notes, Columbine was less a successful school shooting than it was a failed school bombing. Harris, later deemed a psychopath by some psychologists, and Klebold, a suicidal depressive, did not seek out specific groups or individuals. They wanted to blow up the entire place and kill hundreds indiscriminately with a homemade propane bomb. But their device failed to detonate. Only then did they begin using the guns that had unlawfully been supplied to them by others.

Yet the "loner versus bullies" vengeance template came to be widely accepted and applied to later shootings. It can be the sort of facile notion that appeals to those eager for a rational theory to explain an action that is utterly irrational. It can also be unnerving. What high school does not have its share of student bullies and oddballs? Not surprisingly, some parents live in fear that their own children could become tomorrow's victims.

How severe is the threat of school shootings? Certitudes are elusive. Some analyses show an increase over the years, others a decline. One complication is a dearth of research drawing on universally accepted data. Some studies include stabbings in the tally of shootings, or events that occur not on school grounds but nearby, or suicides, or accidental discharges of weapons, or gang fights bearing no resemblance to the Columbine-style massacres that people tend to think of when they hear of school shootings.

Other researchers omit some or all of those categories in chronicling the mayhem. Also, many studies rely heavily on newspaper and television reports, a methodology that may be inherently flawed, given that some situations may well have been overblown by the news media and others ignored.

Retro Report relies on numbers compiled by the Centers for Disease Control and Prevention, based on known school homicides. That standard, too, may be an imperfect guide, but it deals in something tangible that is hard to gainsay: a body count. C.D.C. statistics suggest that shooting homicides in schools have held fairly steady across the last two decades, ranging for the most part between 15 and 30 a year. With well over 100,000 primary and secondary schools in the United States, the odds of any one of them coming under assault seem minuscule.

Some scholars recommend examining school shootings not as a discrete phenomenon but, rather, as one aspect of this country's broader wave of gun violence. One such expert is Dewey G. Cornell, an education professor and forensic clinical psychologist at the University of Virginia. "We have a flood of gun violence in the United States," he told Retro Report, citing an average of more than 300 shootings and 80 deaths a day. "Those occur throughout our community, not just in schools."

For sure, schools must be kept safe, he added, but "we need to think about where that flood is coming from, and address the risk factors and causes of gun violence, rather than focus specifically on the schools."

Risk factors plainly include the easy availability of guns, for the public in general and for the mentally troubled in particular. A debate is also underway over how extensively news organizations should dwell on the details of a mass shooting. That issue has been raised anew with the mass killings this year at a black church in Charleston, S.C., and the fatal shooting of two television journalists during a broadcast in Roanoke, Va. Some propose not even naming the killers, depriving them of the notoriety they seek while perhaps eliminating a possible source of inspiration for would-be copycats.

Then again, all venues are not equal.

New Yorkers, for instance, react more powerfully to a killing in Central Park, their secular cathedral, than to one that takes place just a block or two away; dread and a sense of personal vulnerability touch millions of people. Similarly, terror in a classroom sends shock waves rippling far and wide, whereas slayings at other locations often do not. Even a single school shooting is too much for many people to bear. After all, these are our children.

Columbine Shocked the Nation. Now, Mass Shootings Are Less Surprising.

BY MAGGIE ASTOR | NOV. 10, 2017

WHEN TWO STUDENTS shot up Columbine High School on a sunny Tuesday in 1999, it felt like an earthquake.

There had been school shootings before in the country, including at least six the previous year. But this was the deadliest on record, with 13 people killed, and — perhaps more important psychologically — millions of people across the United States watched it happen on live television. Though it took place in a small town in Colorado, it was experienced as a national calamity. To this day, Columbine endures as an emblem of random, senseless murder. But as of this week, it is no longer one of the 10 deadliest mass shootings in postwar America.

MONICA ALMEIDA/THE NEW YORK TIMES

Students in Littleton, Colo., on April 21, 1999, the day after the mass shooting at Columbine High School.

When it happened, Columbine was the nation's fifth-deadliest mass shooting since World War II, surpassed only by attacks at a Luby's restaurant in Killeen, Tex., in 1991 (23 deaths); at a McDonald's in San Ysidro, Calif., in 1984 (21); at the University of Texas at Austin in 1966 (15); and at a post office in Edmond, Okla., in 1986 (14).

Yet today, not one of those shootings is among the five deadliest. That category, which previously covered more than 30 years, is now occupied entirely by shootings from the past decade — all but one from the past five years.

Fifty-eight people were killed in the Las Vegas shooting. The Orlando nightclub shooting last year, 49. The 2007 Virginia Tech shooting, 32. The 2012 massacre at Sandy Hook Elementary School, 27. As of Sunday, the fifth-deadliest mass shooting since World War II is the attack on a Baptist church in tiny Sutherland Springs, Tex., which killed 26 people.

Columbine was the first mass shooting in nearly eight years that killed 10 or more people — and after 1999, seven years would pass without one. Today, such gaps are unthinkable. Five of the past six years have included at least one shooting with 10 or more casualties.

The American Psychological Association's 2017 "Stress in America" survey found that "violence and crime" was one of the five most common sources of stress in the United States. And people interviewed after mass shootings frequently express a sense that nowhere is safe anymore: not school, not work, not church, not clubs, not concerts, not movie theaters or malls or Walmarts.

But amid the horror and fear, a central emotion seen after Columbine seems to be missing: surprise.

Arthur Evans, chief executive of the American Psychological Association, emphasized that there was no scientific literature on whether public attitudes and reactions to mass shootings had changed. But "anecdotally," he said, "it appears that the public is reacting differently than we did when the events first started happening."

At some point, "How could this happen?" gave way to "Here we go again." The mood is seen in interviews and even in satire: The

Onion has published the same article, headlined " 'No Way to Prevent This,' Says Only Nation Where This Regularly Happens," after six mass shootings.

This is not surprising, Dr. Evans said, given what scientists know about how we react to repeated stimuli.

Studies have shown that when people are exposed to continuous light or sound, "they become less sensitive to that stimuli," he said. "It would be expected that if people are exposed to these kinds of events in the news all the time, that they're going to be less reactive. That wouldn't be surprising at all."

In April 2009, almost exactly 10 years after Columbine, a shooting at an immigrant center in Binghamton, N.Y., killed the same number of people: 13. It came on the heels of a shooting rampage that killed 10 people in rural Alabama in March. But unlike Columbine, it was followed seven months later by yet another mass shooting: this one at Fort Hood, Tex., where a gunman again killed 13 people. And the next eight years brought at least seven shootings with similar or greater death tolls.

Today, the shootings in Binghamton and Alabama are rarely mentioned.

The Virginia Shooter Wanted Fame. Let's Not Give It to Him.

OPINION | BY ZEYNEP TUFEKCI | AUG. 27, 2015

A BRUTAL attack takes place on live television; the on-air reporter and cameraman are fatally shot while at work on an early morning story.

The resulting footage — essentially a stomach-churning snuff film — aired on cable news, and was embedded in online news reports.

In a further grotesque twist, the killer filmed the episode and posted his first-person shooter video on social media. "See Facebook," he tweeted, directing readers to the video that he also posted on Twitter, and which auto-played on many streams as people shared the posts.

This is probably exactly what the shooter, who took two lives and then his own on Wednesday in Virginia, was hoping for in his engineering of mass media and viral infamy. And he is not the only one. Studies show a rise in public mass shootings in the years since the 1999 killings at Columbine High School in Littleton, Colo.

These incidents are often followed by discussions of the availability of guns, and about mental health support. Those are crucial issues. But there is something else going on, too: Many of these shooters are seeking a twisted form of notoriety. The killers' success in obtaining the distorted fame they seek is helping inspire the next troubled person.

We need to understand the copycat aspect of these killings so that we can start dampening this effect.

After studying 160 "active shooter" events over the past decade, with access to information beyond what the public knows, Andre Simons, of the F.B.I.'s Behavioral Analysis Unit, concluded that "the copycat phenomenon is real." When the F.B.I. report summarizing the research was released in 2014, he said: "We think we're seeing more compromised, marginalized individuals who are seeking inspiration from those past attacks."

While we can't know most killers' exact motives, we can study their actions. On the morning he fatally shot two people, the Virginia shooter is believed to have faxed a 23-page document to ABC News. The document lionized other young men who had earlier taken multiple lives — men whose actions, motivations and inspirations had been sensationally documented in the news media. He even compared their "tally" of deaths, praising the Virginia Tech shooter for murdering "double the amount" of the Columbine killers. Like many of these individuals, he seemed deeply interested in ensuring a perverse notoriety for his own brutal acts, as well as for past incidents.

The troubled young man who killed 20 elementary school students in Newtown, Conn., in 2012 meticulously collected news clippings of previous mass killings. The teenager who killed two people in a Maryland shopping mall in 2014 was obsessed with the Columbine massacre — he even waited till the exact time of its occurrence to start shooting. During the trial of the gunman who committed the Aurora, Colo., theater massacre, as news coverage of the event spiked, two more shootings happened in movie theaters in just two weeks. The gunman in Santa Barbara, Calif., who killed six people in 2014 left behind a carefully prepared video screed (which many media outlets played or linked to).

We've long known that media reporting of suicides creates a contagion effect by planting what's known as "the seeds of ideation" in at-risk individuals. Recently, Arizona State University researchers examined whether mass killings and school shootings were similarly contagious. After examining a database of school shootings and mass killings, the researchers reported "significant evidence of contagion." The occurrence of one mass killing meant that another one in the next two weeks was significantly more likely compared with when there had been no such event in the recent past. Crucially, the next one did not necessarily occur nearby, which is what we'd expect if the contagion effect was a result of word-of-mouth or local news. The researchers concluded that high-profile events that got widespread media attention seemed to inspire the next ones.

Psychiatrists agree with the F.B.I.'s conclusion and statistical studies. In 2007, the American Psychiatric Association weighed in, saying that "the scientific evidence in this area is clear." Asking the news media to stop airing the "disturbing writings, photographs and video" of the Virginia Tech killer, the A.P.A. said that publicizing these materials "seriously jeopardizes the public's safety by potentially inciting 'copycat' suicides, homicides and other incidents."

Attention seeking is not a new kind of behavior, but now those who seek attention via infamy have more tools available than ever. They can film their own manifestoes, as did the Virginia Tech shooter, who killed 32 people. They can post their grievances on social media themselves, as did the Santa Barbara shooter, who killed six people. They can even film the shootings from their own vantage point, as Wednesday's live-television shooter did.

These killers act knowing that their ploy is likely to work, and that their faces, words and vicious deeds will be splashed on our screens on their terms.

We can change this by changing the way we cover these stories, similar to the way that the news media did for suicides. After a rash of copycat suicides in the early 1980s, the Centers for Disease Control and Prevention issued voluntary guidelines for reporting on such events: Emphasize that help is possible, do not romanticize the act and do not report on details of the method. (Research shows that being able to imagine an act in specific terms makes it more likely that someone will carry out their plans.)

The media needs to adopt a similar sensible framework to covering mass killings. And in the age of social media, that also means changing our own behavior.

This doesn't mean censoring the news or not reporting important events of obvious news value. It means not providing the killers with the infamy they seek. It means somber, instead of lurid and graphic, coverage, and a focus on victims. It means not putting the killer's face on loop. It means minimizing or not using the killers' names, as I have done here. It means not airing snuff films, or making them easily accessible on popular sites. It means holding back reporting of details such as the type of gun, ammunition, angle of attack and the protective gear the killer might have worn. Such detailed reporting can give the next killer a concrete road map.

This may seem unrealistic. Our media culture tends toward more, not less. But nothing is inevitable, and once awareness of the copycat impact is raised, the news media can change its behavior. It's not true that the media never holds back information or changes its coverage when lives are at stake. Reporting of suicides already generally follows the C.D.C. guidelines. And, back in 2012, when NBC's high-profile foreign correspondent, Richard Engel, was kidnapped in Syria, the fact of the abduction was widely known among journalists. But almost all of them complied with NBC's request for a news blackout to ensure better fact-finding and easier negotiations with the captors. The kidnapping became widely known only after Mr. Engel and his colleagues escaped.

The framework necessary to dampen the copycat effect is nowhere as severe as such a blackout. Instead, it requires not giving the killers the fame they most likely seek for their face or for their words or videos, while reporting on the news with a focus on victims and the brutality of the crime.

For the rest of us, it means not sharing manifestoes or shooters' social media accounts. Such change is possible. Brutal beheadings by the Islamic State used to be covered graphically by the news media, and also shared widely on social media. Recently, each such event in my social media feed has been followed by reminders not to share the videos — and almost nobody in my social network does anymore. Instead, we share pictures from the lives of the victims.

It's true that this material will live on in many places on the Internet, but having to seek it in a seedy corner is different from having it promoted by popular news sites.

Graphic footage may be appropriate at times to shock the conscience toward corrective action, for example with victims of war or state violence. But when a murder is carried out in a way that seems to be courting sensationalized coverage, not publicizing the killer's name, face or screeds is the right response.

These killers seek our attention. It's time we learned how to deny them.

ZEYNEP TUFEKCI IS AN ASSISTANT PROFESSOR AT THE SCHOOL OF INFORMATION AND LIBRARY SCIENCE AT THE UNIVERSITY OF NORTH CAROLINA AND A CONTRIBUTING OPINION WRITER.

CHAPTER 3

Sandy Hook: Redefining the Possibilities of Violence

In 2012, Adam Lanza targeted an elementry school in Newtown, Connecticut — another watershed moment in the history of mass murder in schools. There did not seem to be any rational basis for what Adam Lanza did, and the young age of many of the victims made it all the more difficult to face. If Columbine inaugurated the era of military-style execution, mass murder as vendetta and fame-seeking, then Sandy Hook is a study in the ability of a community to process collective trauma. It was also a catalyst after which parents formed stronger networks to push for stricter gun control.

Nation Reels After Gunman Massacres 20 Children at School in Connecticut

BY JAMES BARRON | DEC. 14, 2012

A 20-YEAR-OLD MAN wearing combat gear and armed with semiautomatic pistols and a semiautomatic rifle killed 26 people — 20 of them children — in an attack in an elementary school in central Connecticut on Friday. Witnesses and officials described a horrific scene as the gunman, with brutal efficiency, chose his victims in two classrooms while other students dove under desks and hid in closets.

Hundreds of terrified parents arrived as their sobbing children were led out of the Sandy Hook Elementary School in a wooded corner of Newtown, Conn. By then, all of the victims had been shot and most were dead, and the gunman, identified as Adam Lanza, had committed suicide. The children killed were said to be 5 to 10 years old.

A 28th person, found dead in a house in the town, was also believed to have been shot by Mr. Lanza. That victim, one law enforcement official said, was Mr. Lanza's mother, Nancy Lanza, who was initially reported to be a teacher at the school. She apparently owned the guns he used.

Although reports at the time indicated that the principal of the school let Mr. Lanza in because she recognized him, his mother did not work at the school, and he shot his way in, defeating a security system requiring visitors to be buzzed in. Moments later, the principal was shot dead when she went to investigate the sound of gunshots. The school psychologist was also among those who died.

The rampage, coming less than two weeks before Christmas, was the nation's second-deadliest school shooting, exceeded only by the 2007 Virginia Tech massacre, in which a gunman killed 32 people and then himself.

Law enforcement officials said Mr. Lanza had grown up in New-town, and he was remembered by high school classmates as smart, introverted and nervous. They said he had gone out of his way not to attract attention when he was younger.

The gunman was chillingly accurate. A spokesman for the State Police said he left only one wounded survivor at the school. All the others hit by the barrage of bullets from the guns Mr. Lanza carried died, suggesting that they were shot at point-blank range. One law enforcement official said the shootings occurred in two classrooms in a section of the single-story Sandy Hook Elementary School.

Some who were there said the shooting occurred during morning announcements, and the initial shots could be heard over the school's public address system. The bodies of those killed were still in the school as of 10 p.m. Friday.

The New York City medical examiner's office sent a "portable morgue" to Newtown to help with the aftermath of the shootings, a spokeswoman, Ellen Borakove, confirmed late Friday.

Law enforcement officials offered no hint of what had motivated Mr. Lanza. It was also unclear, one investigator said, why Mr. Lanza — after shooting his mother to death inside her home — drove her car to the school and slaughtered the children. "I don't think anyone knows the answers to those questions at this point," the official said. As for a possible motive, he added, "we don't know much for sure."

F.B.I. agents interviewed his brother, Ryan Lanza, in Hoboken, N.J. His father, Peter Lanza, who was divorced from Nancy Lanza, was also questioned, one official said.

Newtown, a postcard-perfect New England town where everyone seems to know everyone else and where there had lately been holiday tree lightings with apple cider and hot chocolate, was plunged into mourning. Stunned residents attended four memorial services in the town on Friday evening as detectives continued the search for clues, and an explanation.

Maureen Kerins, a hospital nurse who lives close to the school, learned of the shooting from television and hurried to the school to see if she could help.

"I stood outside waiting to go in, but a police officer came out and said they didn't need any nurses," she said, "so I knew it wasn't good."

In the cold light of Friday morning, faces told the story outside the stricken school. There were the frightened faces of children who were crying as they were led out in a line. There were the grim faces of women. There were the relieved-looking faces of a couple and their little girl.

The shootings set off a tide of anguish nationwide. In Illinois and Georgia, flags were lowered to half-staff in memory of the victims. And at the White House, President Obama struggled to read a statement in the White House briefing room. More than once, he dabbed his eyes.

"Our hearts are broken," Mr. Obama said, adding that his first reaction was not as a president, but as a parent.

"I know there is not a parent in America who does not feel the same overwhelming grief that I do," he said.

He called the victims "beautiful little kids."

"They had their entire lives ahead of them: birthdays, graduations, weddings, kids of their own," he said. Then the president reached up to the corner of one eye.

Mr. Obama called for "meaningful action" to stop such shootings, but he did not spell out details. In his nearly four years in office, he has not pressed for expanded gun control. But he did allude on Friday to a desire to have politicians put aside their differences to deal with ways to prevent future shootings.

Gov. Dannel P. Malloy of Connecticut, who went to Newtown, called the shootings "a tragedy of unspeakable terms."

"Evil visited this community today," he said.

Lt. J. Paul Vance, a spokesman for the Connecticut State Police, described "a very horrific and difficult scene" at the school, which had 700 students in kindergarten through fourth grade. It had a security protocol that called for doors to be locked during the day and visitors to be checked on a video monitor inside.

"You had to buzz in and out and the whole nine yards," said a former chairwoman of the Newtown board of education, Lillian Bittman. "When you buzz, you come up on our screen."

The lock system did not go into effect until 9:30 each morning, according to a letter to parents from the principal, Dawn Hochsprung, that was posted on several news Web sites. The letter was apparently written earlier in the school year.

Lieutenant Vance said the Newtown police had called for help from police departments nearby and began a manhunt, checking "every nook and cranny and every room."

Officers were seen kicking in doors as they worked their way through the school.

Lieutenant Vance said the students who died had been in two classrooms. Others said that as the horror unfolded, students and teachers tried to hide in places the gunman would not think to look. Teachers locked the doors, turned off the lights and closed the blinds. Some ordered students to duck under their desks.

The teachers did not explain what was going on, but they did not have to. Everyone could hear the gunfire.

Yvonne Cech, a school librarian, said she had spent 45 minutes locked in a closet with two library clerks, a library catalog assistant and 18 fourth graders.

"The SWAT team escorted us out," she said, and then the children were reunited with their parents.

Lieutenant Vance said 18 youngsters were pronounced dead at the school and two others were taken to hospitals, where they were declared dead. All the adults who were killed at the school were pronounced dead there.

Law enforcement officials said the weapons used by the gunman were a Sig Sauer and a Glock, both handguns. The police also found a Bushmaster .223 M4 carbine.

One law enforcement official said the guns had not been traced because they had not yet been removed from the school, but state licensing records or permits apparently indicated that Ms. Lanza owned weapons of the same makes and models.

"He visited two classrooms," said a law enforcement official at the scene, adding that those two classrooms were adjoining.

The first 911 call was recorded about 9:30 and said someone had been shot at the school, an almost unthinkable turn of events on what had begun as just another chilly day in quiet Newtown. Soon, frantic parents were racing to the school, hoping their children were all right. By 10:30, the shooting had stopped. By then, the police had arrived with dogs.

"There is going to be a black cloud over this area forever," said Craig Ansman, who led his 4-year-old daughter from the preschool down the street from the elementary school. "It will never go away."

Children Were All Shot Multiple Times With a Semiautomatic, Officials Say

BY JAMES BARRON | DEC. 15, 2012

THE GUNMAN in the Connecticut shooting blasted his way into the elementary school and then sprayed the children with bullets, first from a distance and then at close range, hitting some of them as many as 11 times, as he fired a semiautomatic rifle loaded with ammunition designed for maximum damage, officials said Saturday.

The state's chief medical examiner, H. Wayne Carver II, said all of the 20 children and 6 adults gunned down at Sandy Hook Elementary School in Newtown, Conn., had been struck more than once in the fusillade.

He said their wounds were "all over, all over."

"This is a very devastating set of injuries," he said at a briefing in Newtown. When he was asked if they had suffered after they were hit, he said, "Not for very long."

The disclosures came as the police released the victims' names. They ranged in age from 6 to 56.

The children — 12 girls and 8 boys — were all first-graders. One little girl had just turned 7 on Tuesday. All of the adults were women.

The White House announced that President Obama would visit Newtown on Sunday evening to meet with victims' families and speak at an interfaith vigil

On Saturday, as families began to claim the bodies of lost loved ones, some sought privacy. Others spoke out. Robbie Parker, whose 6-year-old daughter, Emilie, was among the dead, choked back tears as he described her as "bright, creative and very loving."

But, he added, "as we move on from what happened here, what happened to so many people, let us not let it turn into something that defines us."

On a day of anguish and mourning, other details emerged about how, but not why, the devastating attack had happened, turning a place where children were supposed to be safe into a national symbol of heartbreak and horror.

The Newtown school superintendent said the principal and the school psychologist had been shot as they tried to tackle the gunman in order to protect their students.

That was just one act of bravery during the maelstrom. There were others, said the superintendent, Janet Robinson. She said one teacher had helped children escape through a window. Another shoved students into a room with a kiln and held them there until the danger had passed.

MICHAEL APPLETON FOR THE NEW YORK TIMES

Paul Bailo and his son Connor, 12, kneel in front of a sign for the Sandy Hook Elementary School in Newtown, Conn., the day after a mass shooting there.

It was not enough: First responders described a scene of carnage in the two classrooms where the children were killed, with no move ment and no one left to save, everything perfectly still.

The gunman, identified as Adam Lanza, 20, had grown up in Newtown and had an uncle who had been a police officer in New Hampshire. The uncle, James M. Champion, issued a statement expressing "heartfelt sorrow," adding that the family was struggling "to comprehend the tremendous loss we all share."

A spokesman for the Connecticut State Police, Lt. J. Paul Vance, said investigators continued to press for information about Mr. Lanza, and had collected "some very good evidence." He also said that the one survivor of the killings, a woman who was shot and wounded at the school, would be "instrumental" in piecing together what had happened.

But it was unclear why Mr. Lanza had gone on the attack. A law enforcement official said investigators had not found a suicide note or messages that spoke to the planning of such a deadly attack. And Ms. Robinson, the school superintendent, said they had found no connection between Mr. Lanza's mother and the school, in contrast to accounts from authorities on Friday that said she had worked there.

Dr. Carver said it appeared that all of the children had been killed by a "long rifle" that Mr. Lanza was carrying; a .223 Bushmaster semiautomatic rifle was one of the several weapons police found in the school. The other guns were semiautomatic pistols, including a 10-millimeter Glock and a 9-millimeter Sig Sauer.

The bullets Mr. Lanza used were "designed in such a fashion the energy is deposited in the tissue so the bullet stays in," resulting in deep damage, Dr. Carver said. As to how many bullets Mr. Lanza had fired, Dr. Carver said he did not have an exact count. "There were lots of them," he said.

He said that parents had identified their children from photographs to spare them from seeing the gruesome results of the rampage. He said that 4 doctors and 10 technicians had done the autopsies and that he had personally performed seven, all on first-graders.

MICHAEL APPLETON FOR THE NEW YORK TIMES

Lt. J. Paul Vance of the Connecticut State Police, in a news conference Saturday, said the gunman "forced his way" into the school.

"This is probably the worst I have seen or the worst that I know of any of my colleagues having seen," said Dr. Carver, who is 60 and has been Connecticut's chief medical examiner since 1989.

He said that only Mr. Lanza and his first victim — his mother, Nancy Lanza — remained to be autopsied. He said he would do those post-mortems on Sunday.

Officials said the killing spree began early on Friday at the house where the Lanzas lived. There, Mr. Lanza shot his mother in the face, making her his first victim, the authorities said. Then, after taking three guns that belonged to her, they said, he climbed into her car for the short drive to the school.

Outfitted in combat gear, Mr. Lanza shot his way in, defeating a security system requiring visitors to be buzzed in. This contradicted earlier reports that he had been recognized and allowed to enter the one-story building. "He was not voluntarily let into the school at all," Lieutenant Vance said. "He forced his way in."

The lieutenant's account was consistent with recordings of police dispatchers who answered call after call from adults at the school. "The front glass has been broken," one dispatcher cautioned officers who were rushing there, repeating on the police radio what a 911 caller had said on the phone. "They are unsure why."

The dispatchers kept up a running account of the drama at the school. "The individual I have on the phone indicates continuing to hear what he believes to be gunfire," one dispatcher said.

Soon, another dispatcher reported that the "shooting appears to have stopped," and the conversation on the official radios turned to making sure that help was available — enough help.

"What is the number of ambulances you will require?" a dispatcher asked.

The answer hinted at the unthinkable scope of the tragedy: "They are not giving us a number."

Another radio transmission, apparently from someone at the school, underlined the desperation: "You might want to see if the surrounding towns can send E.M.S. personnel. We're running out real quick, real fast."

Inside the school, teachers and school staff members had scrambled to move children to safety as the massacre began. Maryann Jacob, a library clerk, said she initially herded students behind a bookcase against a wall "where they can't be seen." She said that spot had been chosen in practice drills for school lockdowns, but on Friday, she had to move the pupils to a storage room "because we discovered one of our doors didn't lock."

Ms. Jacob said the storage room had crayons and paper that they tore up for the children to color while they waited. "They were asking what was going on," she said. "We said: 'We don't know. Our job is just to be quiet.'" But she said that she did know, because she had called the school office and learned that the school was under siege.

It was eerily silent in the school when police officers rushed in with their rifles drawn. There were the dead or dying in one section of the building, while elsewhere, those who had eluded the bullets were under orders from their teachers to remain quiet in their hiding places.

The officers discovered still more carnage: After gunning down the children and the school employees, the authorities said, Mr. Lanza had killed himself.

The principal, Dawn Hochsprung, 47, and the psychologist, Mary Sherlach, 56, were among the dead, as were the teachers Rachel D'Avino, 29; Anne Marie Murphy, 52; and Victoria Soto, 27. Lauren Rousseau, 30, had started as a full-time teacher in September after years of working as a substitute. "It was the best year of her life," The News-Times quoted her mother, Teresa, a copy editor at the newspaper, as saying.

Ms. Soto reportedly shooed her first graders into closets and cabinets when she heard the first shots, and then, by some accounts, told the gunman the youngsters were in the gym. Her cousin, James Willsie, told ABC News that she had "put herself between the gunman and the kids."

"She lost her life protecting those little ones," he said.

School officials have said there are no immediate plans to reopen Sandy Hook Elementary. Staff members will gather at the high school on Monday to discuss what happened, and students will be assigned to attend other schools by Wednesday.

Dorothy Werden, 49, lives across the street from Christopher and Lynn McDonnell, who lost their daughter Grace, 7, in the rampage. Ms. Werden remembered seeing Grace get on a bus Friday, as she did every morning at 8:45. Shortly afterward, she received a call that there had been a lockdown at the school — something that happens periodically, she said, because there is a prison nearby. It was only when she saw police cars from out of town speed past her that she knew something was seriously wrong.

Like the rest of the nation, she said, local residents were struggling with a single question: Why?

"Why did he have to go to the elementary school and kill all of those defenseless children?" Ms. Werden asked.

'Who Would Do This to Our Poor Little Babies'

BY PETER APPLEBOME AND MICHAEL WILSON | DEC. 14, 2012

NEWTOWN, CONN. — Gradually, the group of frantic parents shrank and was gently ushered to wait in a back room in the old brick firehouse around the corner from Sandy Hook Elementary School.

The sounds of cartoons playing for restless children wafted incongruously through the air, but the adults were hushed. A police officer entered and put the parents' worst fears into words: their children were gone. The wails that followed could be heard from outside, sounding the end of a horrifying shooting that took the lives of 20 children and 6 adults in the school.

It was about 9:30 a.m., when the school locks its doors to the outside world, demanding identification from visitors. What happened next sounded different depending on where you were in the school when a normal school day exploded.

Pops. Bangs. Thundering, pounding booms that echoed, and kept coming and coming. Screams and the cries of children ebbed, until there was only the gunfire.

Countless safety drills learned over generations kicked in. Teachers sprang to their doors and turned the locks tight. Children and adults huddled in closets, crawled under desks and crouched in classroom corners.

Laura Feinstein, a reading support teacher, reached for her telephone. "I called the office and said, 'Barb, is everything O.K.?' and she said, 'There is a shooter in the building.' "

"I heard gunshots going on and on and on," Ms. Feinstein said.

Even in the gym, the loudest room in any school on a given day, something sounded very wrong. "Really loud bangs," said Brendan Murray, 9, who was there with his fourth-grade class. "We thought that someone was knocking something over. And we heard yelling and we heard gunshots. We heard lots of gunshots."

"We heard someone say, " 'Put your hands up!' " Brendan said. "I heard, 'Don't shoot!' We had to go into the closet in the gym."

In the library, Yvonne Cech, a librarian, locked herself, an assistant and 18 fourth graders in a closet behind file cabinets while the sound of gunfire thundered outside.

Witnesses said later that they heard as many as 100 gunshots, but saw next to nothing in their hiding places. What was happening?

"Some people," a little girl said later, searching for words, "they got a stomachache."

The shooting finally stopped. Most teachers kept the children frozen in hiding. Some 15 minutes later, there was another sound, coming from the school intercom. It had been on the whole time. A voice said, "It's O.K. It's safe now."

Brendan, in the gym, said, "Then someone came and told us to run down the hallway. There were police at every door. There were lots of people crying and screaming."

ANDREW SULLIVAN FOR THE NEW YORK TIMES

Children at Sandy Hook Elementary School in Newtown, Conn., crouched in classrooms as a gunman fired as many as 100 shots. Word spread quickly and parents rushed to the scene.

The officers led children past the carnage. "They said 'Close your eyes, hold hands.'" said Vanessa Bajraliu, 9. Outside, a nightmare version of the school was taking shape. Police officers swarmed with dogs and roared overhead in helicopters. There were armored cars and ambulances.

Inside, the librarians and children had been hiding in the closet for 45 minutes when a SWAT team arrived and escorted them out.

Word spread quickly through the small town. At nearby Danbury Hospital, doctors and nurses girded for an onslaught of wounded victims. "We immediately convened four trauma teams to be ready for casualties," a spokeswoman, Andrea Rynn, said. Nurses, surgeons, internal medicine and imaging specialists, as well as staff members from pathology and the hospital lab, rushed to assemble in the emergency room to receive an influx of patients from the shooting. An influx that never arrived. Only three victims came to the hospital, two of whom did not survive. The rest were already dead.

"I've been here for 11 years," Ms. Feinstein, the teacher, said. "I can't imagine who would do this to our poor little babies."

Another nurse who lives near the school hurried to the scene. "But a police officer came out and said they didn't need any nurses," she said. "So I knew it wasn't good."

Survivors gathered at the Sandy Hook Volunteer Fire and Rescue station house, just down the street. Parents heard — on the radio, or on television, or via text messages or calls from an automated, emergency service phone tree — and came running. In the confusion, there were shrieks of joy as mothers and fathers were reunited with their children.

The parents whose children were unaccounted for were taken to the separate room, and a list of the missing was made. The pastor of St. Rose of Lima Church, Msgr. Robert Weiss, saw the list. "It was around, obviously, the number that passed away," he said.

The Rev. Matthew Crebbin of Newtown Congregational Church was there, too.

The police in Newtown searched houses near the school.

"It's very agonizing for the families, but they are trying to be very meticulous," he said. "But it is very difficult for people."

A woman named Diane, a friend of a parent whose child was missing, said a state trooper had been assigned to each family. "I think there are 20 sets of parents over there," she said.

In another room of the firehouse, there were the oddly joyous sounds of the cartoons. There were plates and pans of pizza and other donated food. No one touched it.

"There was a multifaith service with people sitting in folding chairs in a circle," said John Woodall, a psychiatrist who lives nearby and went to the firehouse. "And after that, people milled around and waited for news."

Outside, reunions continued. News, good and bad, was borne on the faces of the people around the school. Three women emerged with their arms around the one in the middle, protecting her. "We just want to get her home," one said.

A few minutes later, a mother and father practically ran past in relief, a little girl in a light blue jacket riding on her father's shoulders.

Brendan's father had been at home about a mile away with his wife when the phone rang, a call from the automated alert system saying there was a lockdown at the school.

"At first we weren't too nervous, because you hear of lockdowns happening all the time," said his father, Sean Murray. "Like if there was a liquor store down here being robbed, all the schools would go into lockdown."

They turned on the television and heard about the shooting, and how parents were being advised to stay away from the school. They ran to the car and went, and found Brendan waiting.

"It's sick," Mr. Murray said. "It's sick that something like this could happen at an elementary school."

Bonnie Fredericks, the owner of Sandy Hook Hair Company, said that many of the town's children had gathered recently for the lighting of the village Christmas tree, down the street from her shop.

Twenty were gone now. "We'll know all of them," she said.

Beside her shop, a sandwich board outside a liquor store relayed a simple message, pasted over a sign advertising a beer special: "Say a prayer."

Nation's Pain Is Renewed, and Difficult Questions Are Asked Once More

BY WILLIAM GLABERSON | DEC. 14, 2012

ON FRIDAY, as Newtown, Conn., joined the list of places like Littleton, Colo., and Jonesboro, Ark., where schools became the scenes of stunning violence, the questions were familiar: Why does it happen? What can be done to stop it?

The questions have emerged after all of the mass killings in recent decades — at a Virginia college campus, a Colorado movie theater, a Wisconsin temple — but they took on an added sting when the victims included children.

The fact that the Newtown massacre, with 26 killed at the school, along with the gunman, was the second deadliest school shooting in the country's history — after the 32 people killed at Virginia Tech in 2007 — once again made this process of examination urgent national business as details emerged from Sandy Hook Elementary School.

This painful corner of modern American history does offer some answers: Many of the mass killers had histories of mental illness, with warning signs missed by the people who knew them and their sometimes clear signs of psychological deterioration left unaddressed by the country's mental health system.

The shootings almost always renew the debate about access to guns, and spur examination of security practices and missed warning signals in what were damaged lives.

Research on mass school killings shows that they are exceedingly rare. Amanda B. Nickerson, director of a center that studies school violence and abuse prevention at the University at Buffalo, said studies made clear that American schools were quite safe and that children were more likely to be killed outside of school.

But, she said, events like the Sandy Hook killings trigger fundamental fears. "When something like this happens," she said, "everybody says it's an epidemic, and that's just not true."

Dylan Klebold, 17, and Eric Harris, 18, may have earned singular infamy with the killing of 12 other students and a teacher from Columbine High School, in Littleton, Colo., in 1999, but there have been others who breached the safety of American schoolhouses over the decades.

In 1927, a school board official in Bath, Mich., killed 44 people, including students and teachers, when he blew up the town's school.

Even before Columbine in the late 1990s, school shootings seemed to be a national scourge, with killings in places like Jonesboro, Ark., and Springfield, Ore. In 2006, a 32-year-old man shot 11 girls at an Amish school in Nickel Mines, Pa., killing 5 of them.

Often in a haze of illness, the schoolhouse gunmen are usually aware of the taboo they are breaking by targeting children, said Dewey G. Cornell, a clinical psychologist at the University of Virginia and director of the Virginia Youth Violence Project. "They know it's a tremendous statement that shocks people," Dr. Cornell said, "and that is a reflection of their tremendous pain and their drive to communicate that pain."

After 14-year-old Michael Carneal opened fire on a prayer group at Heath High School in West Paducah, Ky., in 1997, it came out that he had made no secret of his plans. "He told me, once or twice, that he thought it would be cool to walk — or run — down the halls shooting people," a friend from the school band testified later. Five Heath students were wounded; three were killed.

But some experts on school violence said Friday that it was not so much the character of the relatively rare schoolhouse gunman as it was the public perception of the shootings that transformed them into national and even international events. Dunblane, Scotland, is remembered for the day in 1996 when a 43-year-old man stormed a gym class of 5- and 6-year-olds, killing 16 children and a teacher.

Over the years there have been some indications of what warning signs to look for. The New York Times published an analysis in 2000 of what was known about 102 people who had committed 100 rampage killings at schools, job sites and public places like malls.

Most had left a road map of red flags, plotting their attacks and accumulating weapons. In the 100 rampage killings reviewed, 54 of the killers had talked explicitly of when and where they would act, and against whom. In 34 of the cases, worried friends or family members had desperately sought help in advance, only to be rebuffed by the police, school officials or mental health workers.

After the deaths in Sandy Hook on Friday, there was new talk of the need to be vigilant. But there has also been talk of the sober reality that it is hard to turn the ordinary places of life into fortresses.

Dr. Irwin Redlener, who is the director of the National Center for Disaster Preparedness at Columbia University and has worked on school violence issues, said there were steps that could be taken to try to limit school violence, like limiting entry, developing an explicit disaster plan that includes strategies to lock down schools and pursuing close ties with the local police.

"Unfortunately," he said, "random acts of severe violence like this are not possible to entirely prevent."

After Sandy Hook, More Than 400 People Have Been Shot in Over 200 School Shootings

BY JUGAL K. PATEL | FEB. 15, 2018

WHEN A GUNMAN killed 20 first graders and six adults with an assault rifle at Sandy Hook Elementary School in 2012, it rattled Newtown, Conn., and reverberated across the world. Since then, there have been at least 239 school shootings nationwide. In those episodes, 438 people were shot, 138 of whom were killed.

The data used here is from the Gun Violence Archive, a nonprofit that began tracking school shootings in 2014, about a year after Sandy Hook.

The shootings have taken place at sporting events and in parking lots, cafeterias, hallways and classrooms.

A shooting took place Wednesday at Marjory Stoneman Douglas High School in Parkland, Fla., about an hour northwest of Miami. As of Wednesday night, 17 people had been killed and the number of people injured was unknown.

Sixteen of the 239 shootings shown below can be classified as mass shootings, events in which four or more people are shot.

On average, there have been about five school shootings each month, including episodes that were not mass shootings.

Each of the episodes falls under the definition of "school shooting" used by the Gun Violence Archive.

The nonprofit defines a school shooting as an episode on the property of an elementary school, secondary school or college campus. Another defining characteristic is timing — shootings must occur during school hours or during extracurricular activities.

Only episodes in which people were injured or killed by gunfire are included. Injuries like a leg broken while fleeing the site were not archived.

Police reports often leave out the origin of guns used in school shootings, but researchers say a significant portion of the guns used in such episodes come from the shooters' homes.

Many children have access to unlocked guns at home. Data from gun ownership surveys conducted by the Pew Research Center show that 54 percent of gun owners with children under 18 living at home say they keep all of their guns locked away.

Fourteen states and Washington, D.C., have laws that impose criminal liability on those who store guns at home and know "or reasonably should know" that those firearms are accessible to children.

In a study conducted in 2000 by the RAND Corporation, researchers estimated that more than 22 million children live in homes with a firearm.

CHAPTER 4

Parkland: New Tragedy, New Politics

While school shootings have become horrifyingly repetitive, the politics of guns has changed in the polarized and energized political atmosphere of the Trump era. Mass murder in Parkland, Florida, reanimated the debate around access to guns and mental health services. But new controversies arose about how police should behave when confronting a danger to the public, how students and parents ought to react to tragedy, the role of the media in processing national tragedy and the obligation that leaders have to take action when it is warranted.

As Shots Ring Out, a Student Texts: 'If I Don't Make It, I Love You'

BY AUDRA D. S. BURCH AND PATRICIA MAZZEI | FEB. 14, 2018

PARKLAND, FLA. — One student hit her record button while being led out of the school to safety by sheriff's deputies. On her way, her cellphone's shaking camera lens passed over several bodies sprawled on the floor.

In another cellphone video, several dozen gunshots were audible not far away. "Oh my God! Oh my God!" one student shouted.

Like many school districts, Broward County's allows high school students to bring cellphones to school, so long as they don't interfere with class work. On Wednesday, many students at Marjory Stoneman Douglas High School held onto their phones for dear life as a 19-year-old gunman, Nikolas Cruz, stalked the grounds and fatally shot 17 people. They used them to keep their terrified parents informed about what was happening. And they used them to keep a visual record of an awful crime.

Sarah Crescitelli, a freshman, was in drama class rehearsing for a coming run of the musical "Yo, Vikings," when gunshots rang out

Hiding in a sweltering storage room with about 40 other students, she typed out a text message to her mother, Stacy, for what she thought might be the last time.

"If I don't make it," she wrote, "I love you and I appreciate everything you did for me."

Some of the alarming videos of the mass shooting were passed around via text message, while others quickly made their way to Twitter, where they triggered "sensitive material" warnings.

One video showed officers with guns drawn, rushing into a classroom full of cowering students. The officers told students to put up their hands. One officer bellowed: "Put your phones away! Put your phones away!"

"THE SAFEST COMMUNITY IN THE COUNTY"

Parkland is the type of community where affluent young parents move to find verdant parks and pristine sidewalks for their children. Most everybody knows somebody at Stoneman Douglas High, home of the Eagles.

A famous alumnus of M.S.D., as the school is widely known, is Anthony Rizzo, who plays first base for the Chicago Cubs. Sheriff Scott Israel, who was briefing journalists on the tragedy inside the school, has triplets who graduated from M.S.D. and played football and lacrosse and ran track there. Sheriff Israel said one of his deputies had learned that his son had been injured in the attack.

State Representative Jared Moskowitz, who graduated from M.S.D. in 1999, sends his 4-year-old to a preschool down the street.

The high school, with more than 3,000 students, is almost a city within a city, with airy breezeways and an open courtyard. It bears the name of Stoneman Douglas, the famed environmentalist who crusaded against paving over the Everglades.

"It's surreal," Mr. Moskowitz said. "People don't come to Parkland to open a business. They come to Parkland to raise a family. They come to Parkland to send their child to an A-rated school. They come to Parkland to live in the safest community in the county."

A DAY THAT BEGAN WITH "LIFE"

Every morning at Stoneman Douglas High begins with an affirmation, which is read over the intercom. On Wednesday morning, the affirmation began with the word life.

"Life supports me in every way possible" were the first words students heard that day.

The announcement went on to speak of Valentine's Day, and how everyone "deserves a safe and healthy relationship."

The Astronomy Club announced that it was celebrating Black History Month on Thursday night with a showing of the movie "Hidden Figures." But that event was postponed, as Stoneman Douglas canceled all school events and called in grief counselors.

THE DRILL THAT WASN'T

Melissa Falkowski was teaching a journalism class when the fire alarm went off at about 2:30 p.m. It had been activated shortly before the shots began, perhaps an effort by the gunman to sow confusion.

And it was the second time the alarm went off Wednesday, after a fire alarm earlier in the day.

"Everyone is annoyed because we'd already had one today," she said. "It's unusual but it's not unheard-of, because sometimes someone in culinary burns something and it might go off three times in a day."

There also had been a drill a few weeks before: an active-shooter drill, the kind many schools now do.

Dutifully, Ms. Falkowski followed the fire drill protocol and filed her students out of the classroom to their appointed gathering spot. One of the school's security officers told her: "No, it's a code red. Go back."

In geometry class, Gabriella Figueroa, 16, a junior, had been working on angle bisectors when the alarm sounded. As she neared the exit doors, she heard the first gunshots and ran back to class. "I was shaking and praying and saying, 'God, please get me out of here,'" she said.

Ms. Falkowski took 20 students into a closet reserved for photo gear. Some of the students began to sob, but most stayed quiet, texting in the dark. It got so hot that they had to crack the door open periodically to get enough air.

Finally, after 35 minutes, they heard noises inside the classroom, and then a voice: "This is the police. Is anyone in here?"

The shooting had happened in a different building. None of them had heard gunfire.

Most of the 17 children and adults who died remained unidentified by the authorities as of Wednesday night. One of the complications, the sheriff said, was that the students' identifications were still in their backpacks, which they had left behind in the havoc.

The Names and Faces of the Florida School Shooting Victims

BY JESS BIDGOOD, AMY HARMON, MITCH SMITH AND MAYA SALAM | FEB. 15, 2018

AS GUNSHOTS ECHOED through the high school, a geography teacher, Scott Beigel, 35, paused to usher stragglers into his classroom before locking the door, only to be shot and killed himself as the shooter strode by.

A parent, Jennifer Zeif, credited Mr. Beigel for saving her son's life. Her son, Matthew, 14, had been the last one to slip inside the class, just ahead of Mr. Beigel. Seconds later, the room filled with a smoky haze, Matthew said, and he turned to see his teacher lying near the door, pale and bleeding.

"Mr. Beigel could have passed Matthew up and gone in the classroom first," Ms. Zeif said. "In that case, Matthew would have been the one in the doorway."

On Thursday, as officials identified 17 people killed in the shooting at Marjory Stoneman Douglas High School in Parkland, Fla., some of the victims, like Mr. Beigel, were remembered for having tried to spare others in the moments of chaos that unfolded inside the school.

Aaron Feis, a popular football coach who was killed, also had tried to protect students, officials said. "He was that kind of guy," said Jack Fris, a former football player at the school.

Friends said they were not surprised that Mr. Beigel, a much-beloved figure at a Pennsylvania summer camp that he attended and later helped to run, had put his students' safety above his own.

"Thousands of people at Camp Starlight looked up to Scott," said Grant Williams, 33, an emergency room nurse who worked with Mr. Beigel at the camp for several summers and was mourning long-distance with former camp counselors and campers on Thursday. "He was someone you strive to be like," said another former Starlight counselor.

At the Florida high school, teachers and students were among the dead. There was a soccer player, a student nicknamed Guac and a trombonist in the marching band. Eight of the victims were girls and young women; nine were boys and men. They ranged from 14 years old to 49.

These are some of their stories.

ALYSSA ALHADEFF

Alyssa Alhadeff, 14, had played competitive soccer since she was 3 years old. Like any athlete, she had her ups and downs. But when her club, Parkland, faced off against the rival team from Coral Springs on Feb. 13, she was at the top of her game.

"Her passing was on, her shooting was on, her decision-making was on," her mother, Lori Alhadeff, recalled. With her outgoing personality, Alyssa had a wide circle of friends at Marjory Stoneman Douglas High School. She placed first in a debate tournament, was taking Algebra 2 and Spanish 3, and was honing her skills as an attacking midfielder. The score at what was to be her last time on the soccer field was 1-0, Parkland.

"I was so proud of her," her mother said. "I told her it was the best game of her life."

MARTIN DUQUE ANGUIANO

Martin Duque Anguiano, a 14-year-old freshman, was "a very funny kid, outgoing and sometimes really quiet," his brother, Miguel Duque, wrote on a GoFundMe page for funeral expenses.

"He was sweet and caring and loved by all his family," Miguel wrote. "Most of all he was my baby brother."

NICHOLAS DWORET

Nicholas Dworet, a promising high school swimmer, took a recruiting visit to the University of Indianapolis a few weeks ago. After a group dinner, he pulled the coach aside and said he wanted to compete there after he graduated this spring.

"He was an instant part of our family," said Jason Hite, the university's swim coach. Mr. Hite said Nicholas, 17, had received an academic scholarship and planned to study physical therapy.

University officials and a youth swim team in Florida said Nicholas was among those killed on Wednesday. A post on the Facebook page for TS Aquatics, the Florida club where he swam, described Nicholas as an amazing person who had been "on a major upswing in his life."

Nicholas had improved academically and athletically since starting high school, Mr. Hite said, and his mentors in Florida "felt like the best was still to come for him."

"We were going to continue to groom him to be a future leader for our team," Mr. Hite said.

Mr. Hite said he sent Nicholas a text message on Wednesday afternoon after hearing about the shooting at his school. He got no response.

"The saddest thing to me is how much life this kid had and how hard he had worked to change directions and change paths," Mr. Hite said. "He was really going in the right direction and he had really created some opportunities for himself."

AARON FEIS

At Stoneman Douglas, Mr. Feis was known to all — an assistant football coach and a security monitor. But he too had graduated from the school, played on the football team, and knew exactly what it was like to be a student in these halls.

So he was seen as someone who looked out for students who got in trouble, those who were struggling, those without fathers at home. "They said he was like another father," Mr. Feis's grandfather, Raymond, recalled. "He'd go out of his way to help anybody."

School officials said that Mr. Feis, 37, did the same on Wednesday. When there were signs of trouble, they said, he responded immediately to help. "When Aaron Feis died, when he was killed — tragically, inhumanely — he did it protecting others; you can guarantee that," said Scott Israel, the sheriff of Broward County.

"I don't know when Aaron's funeral is," Sheriff Israel said. "I don't know how many adults are going to go, but you'll get 2,000 kids there."

In Parkland, Austin Lazar, a student, recalled his former coach as cheery and selfless. "He always put everybody before himself."

Mr. Feis was married, his family said, and had a daughter, Arielle.

JAIME GUTTENBERG

Jaime Guttenberg, 14, danced nonstop. Sometimes she went on for hours, her aunt, Ellyn Guttenberg, said. Jaime was warm, too, always taking Ms. Guttenberg's son, who has special needs, under her wing.

Jaime's Facebook page, now memorialized, shows photos of her dancing, hanging out with friends, enjoying the beach and snuggling a dog.

Her father, Fred Guttenberg, posted this on Facebook: "I am broken as I write this trying to figure out how my family gets through this."

CHRISTOPHER HIXON

Christopher Hixon, 49, the school's athletic director, was a well-known figure in Florida high school sports. One man, Jose Roman, posted on social media that Mr. Hixon was "a great coach and an awesome motivator" when he was a freshman athlete years ago.

Mr. Hixon was named athletic director of the year in 2017 by the Broward County Athletics Association.

LUKE HOYER

Luke Hoyer, 15, spent last Christmas with his extended family in South Carolina, where he bowled, joined in a big holiday meal and swapped stories with relatives.

A cousin, Grant Cox, who was at the Christmas gathering said the family had been told by the police that Luke, a freshman at Stoneman Douglas, was among those killed on Wednesday.

Mr. Cox said Luke was a basketball player who was ambitious about the sport and admired N.B.A. stars like LeBron James and Stephen Curry.

"I know Luke loved his family," Mr. Cox said. "I know he did. He had a huge heart."

"He was quiet, but a very happy individual," he said.

CARA LOUGHRAN

Cara Loughran, 14, loved the beach. She adored her cousins. And she was an excellent student, her family said.

"We are absolutely gutted," by her death, her aunt, Lindsay Fontana, wrote in a Facebook post. "While your thoughts are appreciated, I beg you to DO SOMETHING. This should not have happened to our niece Cara and it cannot happen to other people's families."

GINA MONTALTO

Gina Montalto, 14, was identified in local news accounts as a member of her school's winter color guard team.

Andy Mroczek, who has worked as a choreographer at Stoneman Douglas, posted a tribute to Gina on Facebook. "We lost a beautiful soul tonight," he wrote.

JOAQUIN OLIVER

People often spelled Joaquin Oliver's first name wrong, so he went with a snappy nickname: Guac.

He played basketball in the city recreational league — his jersey number was 2 — and he loved to write, filling a notebook with poetry, said Julien Decoste, a close friend of Joaquin's and a fellow senior at Stoneman Douglas.

"Guac and I always wanted to graduate together and prove everyone wrong, that we would be successful together," Julien said.

On Tuesday, Joaquin, 17, asked Julien to help out at his next basketball game, which was scheduled for Thursday.

"I'll be there," Julien texted his friend. "Good looks brotha," Joaquin responded.

On Wednesday, as he hid inside a closet during the shooting, Julien texted Joaquin to check in.

"You good?" Julien texted. "Bro I need you to answer me please."

ALAINA PETTY

Alaina Petty, 14, had helped do cleanup work in Florida after Hurricane Irma, her family said in a statement, and she was an active member of a volunteer group with the Church of Jesus Christ of Latter-day Saints.

"Her selfless service brought peace and joy to those that had lost everything during the storm," the family's statement said. "While we will not have the opportunity to watch her grow up and become the amazing woman we know she would become, we are keeping an eternal perspective."

Alaina was also a member of the Junior Reserve Officer Training Corps, her family said.

MEADOW POLLACK

Meadow Pollack, 18, was a senior at the high school who was planning to go to Lynn University in Boca Raton, Fla., next year, according to her father, Andrew Pollack, who said his daughter was among the dead.

"She was just unbelievable," Mr. Pollack said. "She was a very strong-willed young girl who had everything going for her."

Mr. Pollack described his daughter as smart, beautiful and caring. She worked at her boyfriend's family's motorcycle repair business.

"She just knew how to get what she wanted all the time," Mr. Pollack said. "Nothing could ever stop her from what she wanted to achieve."

HELENA RAMSAY

Helena Ramsay, 17, was smart, kindhearted and thoughtful, her relative, Curtis Page, wrote on Facebook.

"Though she was somewhat reserved, she had a relentless motivation towards her academic studies, and her soft warm demeanor brought the best out in all who knew her," he said, later adding: "She would have started college next year."

ALEX SCHACHTER

Alex Schachter, 14, played the trombone in the Stoneman Douglas marching band, and was proud to have participated in winning a state championship last year. A freshman at the high school, he often played basketball with friends and was "a sweetheart of a kid," his father, Max Schachter, said. Earlier this week, the two had discussed which classes Alex would take next semester.

Mr. Schachter said Alex had loved his mother, who died when he was five years old. His older brother also attends Stoneman Douglas and survived the shooting. Alex "just wanted to do well and make his parents happy," his father said.

CARMEN SCHENTRUP

Carmen Schentrup, a 2018 National Merit Scholarship semifinalist, was the smartest 16-year-old that her cousin, Matt Brandow, had ever met, he said in a Facebook post.

"I'm in a daze right now," he wrote.

PETER WANG

Peter Wang, 15, a freshman, helped his cousin, Aaron Chen, adjust when he settled in Florida.

"He was always so nice and so generous," Aaron, 16, said, adding that even though Peter was younger he had worked to be sure Aaron didn't get bullied when he first arrived.

Peter was last seen in his gray uniform for the Junior Reserve Officer Training Corps, or J.R.O.T.C., on Wednesday. On Thursday, Aaron and another cousin said the authorities had informed the family that Peter was among those killed in the shooting.

"He was the kid in school who would be friends with anyone," said the other cousin, Lin Chen, 24. "He didn't care about popularity."

Reporting on a Mass Shooting, Again

BY ALEXANDRIA SYMONDS AND RAILLAN BROOKS | FEB. 16, 2018

FOR A RECENT ESSAY, Dan Barry explores a difficult question: What are Americans to make of the routine we've developed when it comes to reacting to mass shootings?

It's a question journalists ask themselves, too — and one that informs The Times's coverage of these events on the deepest level. When shootings happen as often as they do, "there is a certain similarity to the journalistic script," said the National editor, Marc Lacey. Reporters know where to go and what to ask, and some themes recur from shooting to shooting.

But the logistical playbook isn't an emotional one, he emphasized: "Our job is to never allow this to become routine, and to, once we do confirm it, react and cover it aggressively, as though it's the very first one we've covered."

The National desk receives reports of active gunman situations in the United States at least once a day, Mr. Lacey said, which percolate among many dozens of stories The Times considers in pursuit of the news that will drive the day. Early Wednesday afternoon, as reports of a potential active gunman at Marjory Stoneman Douglas High School in Parkland, Fla., began to surface on social media, reporters and editors monitored the situation and began to try to confirm details.

The Times's Miami bureau chief, Patricia Mazzei, began making calls, while a correspondent, Audra D. S. Burch, and a stringer, Nick Madigan, were dispatched to the school. By 3:30 p.m., when the front-page meeting is held, editors had the sense it was likely to lead Thursday's paper. Then came the work of putting together three initial stories: the straightforward news piece, a profile of the suspect and an article on the scene in Parkland.

"The National desk didn't hand off the story to other editors until well past midnight," Mr. Lacey said. "We were here again maybe five, six hours later, starting up again." By early Thursday afternoon, less than 24 hours after the shooting, he estimated at least 25 reporters and 15 editors were working on the story.

Elsewhere in the newsroom on Wednesday, the video and graphics teams began spinning up. Steve Duenes, an assistant managing editor and head of the Graphics desk, said that in breaking news events, the team starts by focusing on the scene.

Within about an hour of learning the news, the team generated a locator map, which they then detailed with new information as reporters acquired it. The aim, Mr. Duenes explained, was to offer as much context as possible; because of a grim coincidence, they had something of a head start this time around. The Graphics department was already working on a piece about the more than 200 school shootings since the Sandy Hook massacre in 2012. They rushed to publish that story, he said, "to help readers understand the consistency of the events, the scale."

Video team producers watched while the full sweep of the attack came into view. But, helped by the ubiquity of recording technology and smartphones, they could begin pulling in visuals right away. "We were looking at how people were evacuated, and it seemed like half of the students were filming it," said Mark Schleffler, the department's news director. The first Times video went up in under two hours — one of their faster turnarounds. "One of the lessons we've learned is that people just want to know what happened," Mr. Schleffler said. "We try to just capture the visceral moment on a first pass."

The Express desk, a general assignment team that helps other desks with breaking news reporting and editing, monitored television broadcasts and social media feeds for more developments. Twitter, especially, can be a fruitful source of details — but also a dangerous one, susceptible to being clouded by misinformation, both unintentional and not. "I start with the basic assumption that everything I'm seeing is wrong, old or fake — and thus unusable," said Daniel Victor, an Express reporter. "Then I work toward proving that it's genuine, only then considering it for publication."

The immediate journalistic demands of covering a mass shooting are obvious: Gather as much information as possible, confirm it, convey it. What happens several days later, and in the following weeks, is less so; balancing on-the-spot reporting with deeper, more time-consuming analysis is a key concern. "We're going to have a presence in this town for some time," Mr. Lacey said of Parkland. "We're not going to just disappear tomorrow. The New York Times tends to want to be one of the first people there and one of the last to go." Given the similarities from shooting to shooting, it sometimes makes sense for the digital team to resurface material — on social media, the home page or both — The Times ran on previous occasions. On Thursday, a 2016 story by C. J. Chivers about the military-style weapons often used in mass shootings, including Wednesday's, was of interest once again to readers. So were two Opinion pieces published after the Las Vegas shooting last year: one by Nicholas D. Kristof, suggesting several policy measures to curb gun violence; the other listing the top Congressional recipients of donations by the National Rifle Association.

The repetition wears on journalists just as it wears on everyone. "Nobody enjoys covering mass shootings. Nobody does," Mr. Lacey said. "Every American feels helpless about these awful incidents."

But, he added, he hopes the journalists he leads feel proud of their role in informing the public. "That's your role in perhaps changing society," he said, "by letting people know what actually occurred."

'How Did This Happen?': Grief and Fury After Florida Shooting

BY JULIE TURKEWITZ, PATRICIA MAZZEI AND AUDRA D. S. BURCH | FEB. 16, 2018

PARKLAND, FLA. — Grief and raw anger were palpable on Friday at the first funerals for students who died in one of the deadliest shootings in modern American history earlier this week.

"You," said Andrew Pollack, directing his fury at the man who authorities have identified as the gunman who killed his daughter, Meadow Pollack, 18. "Killed. My. Kid. My kid is dead. It goes through my head all day. And night."

As the burials began for the 17 victims, the F.B.I. acknowledged that it had failed to act on a warning last month that Nikolas Cruz, the suspect in Wednesday's shooting, might kill people at a school. On Friday evening, President Trump and the first lady, Melania Trump, made an unannounced visit to meet with law enforcement officials and medical workers who helped in the wake of the shooting.

The consequences from the shooting have reverberated far beyond school, Marjory Stoneman Douglas High in Parkland, Fla., as schools around the nation closed Friday, or canceled activities after receiving threats. A teacher in Denver said she moved items from a closet in her classroom "to make more space for 9-year-olds to hide."

HERE'S THE LATEST:

- Mr. Cruz is being held without bond at the Broward County jail, where he has been placed on suicide watch, according to Gordon Weekes, the county's chief assistant public defender. He faces 17 counts of premeditated murder.

- A federal law enforcement official on Friday said that Mr. Cruz fired more than 100 rounds during the shooting.

- Sheriff Scott Israel of Broward County said that his office had received about 20 calls about Mr. Cruz over the past two years, though cautioned that some of the calls may not have resulted in a response by officers.

• More than 2,000 students have been interviewed as part of the investigation, the sheriff said. He added that Mr. Cruz did not have a gas mask or smoke grenades, as had previously been reported.

• In Florida, an AR-15 is easier to buy than a handgun.

FLORIDA'S GOVERNOR CALLS ON THE F.B.I. DIRECTOR TO RESIGN.

The F.B.I.'s admission that it failed to act on a tip in January from a person close to Mr. Cruz prompted Gov. Rick Scott of Florida to call for the bureau's director to resign.

The bureau, which was already under considerable political pressure because of its investigation into Mr. Trump, faced calls for even more scrutiny following the massacre.

Mr. Scott said that Christopher A. Wray, the director of the F.B.I., should step down and that the bureau's failure to act on the tip about Mr. Cruz was "unacceptable." "Seventeen innocent people are dead and acknowledging a mistake isn't going to cut it," Mr. Scott said in a statement.

In an unusually sharp public rebuke of his own agents, Attorney General Jeff Sessions said Friday that the missed warnings had "tragic consequences" and that "the F.B.I. in conjunction with our state and local partners must act flawlessly to prevent all attacks. This is imperative, and we must do better."

Robert F. Lasky, the special agent in charge of the F.B.I. field office in Miami, said the agency advised the victims' parents about the misstep in a conference call on Friday.

"We will be looking into where and how the protocol broke down," he said.

"HOW DOES THIS HAPPEN?" A PARENT ASKS AS VICTIMS' FUNERALS BEGIN.

At the first funeral, Alyssa Miriam Alhadeff, 14, was remembered for her joy and kindness, traits that had attracted a wide circle of friends. Hundreds of mourners filled the Star of David Funeral Chapel in North Lauderdale, Fla., spilling outside.

Among the youngest victims, Alyssa, an honor student and a player for the Parkland soccer club, was buried in the Garden of Aaron at Star of David Memorial Gardens.

Her mother, Lori Alhadeff, urged Alyssa's friends to stay in touch, but also let their future success be her daughter's legacy. "Live, breathe for Alyssa," she said.

At a synagogue just a mile from where she had been gunned down, Meadow Pollack, 18, lay in a plain wooden coffin, closed in accordance with Jewish tradition.

Before her were hundreds of mourners, seated in row upon row and crowding every wall and corner: her cousins, her classmates, the governor and so many others. She is survived by many family members, including her brothers and her grandmother Evelyn.

Her father stood in a black suit before the crowd.

"How does this happen to my beautiful, smart, loving daughter?" Mr. Pollack said. "She is everything. If we could learn one thing from this tragedy, it's that our everythings are not safe when we send them to school."

The room heaved with sobbing teenagers, and mourners wheeled out Ms. Pollack's coffin, to be buried in a nearby cemetery.

"IT'S SAD SOMETHING LIKE THAT COULD HAPPEN," THE PRESIDENT SAID IN FLORIDA.

The Trumps arrived Friday evening at a hospital in Pompano Beach that took in eight of the shooting victims, accompanied by John F. Kelly, the White House chief of staff, and Senator Marco Rubio, Republican of Florida.

The president and Mrs. Trump visited the Broward Health North Hospital "to pay their respects and thank the medical professionals for their life-saving assistance," according to a statement related by a White House spokeswoman on Friday evening.

When asked if he met with victims, Mr. Trump said: "Yes, I did. I did indeed."

"It's sad something like that could happen," he said.

Mr. Trump did not respond when he was asked if gun laws needed to be changed. He then walked into another room.

Later, speaking during a meeting with law enforcement officials at the Broward County sheriff's office, the president thanked first responders for what he called an "incredible job," according to a White House press pool report.

Mr. Trump said he had met with the parents of some of the victims, and also spoke with a female victim at the hospital who he said had been shot four times and was saved because emergency workers got her to the hospital quickly.

SCHOOLS ACROSS THE NATION ARE ON EDGE AFTER WEDNESDAY'S SHOOTING.

The authorities were still investigating reports of shots fired on Friday morning at Highline College, about half an hour's drive south of Seattle, said Capt. Kyle Ohashi, a spokesman for the Puget Sound Regional Fire Authority. No physical evidence of a weapons discharge — including shell casings or damage to any structure — had been found, he said. The school said in a statement on Facebook that the situation was cleared about three hours after a lockdown began. Several other agencies, including the federal Bureau of Alcohol Tobacco, Firearms and Explosives, had also responded.

The Gilchrist County School District in Florida shuttered its schools after receiving an email threat, and the Nutley Public School System in New Jersey also said it would be closed because of a security threat. A high school in Colorado Springs canceled a pep rally.

Schools also wrestled with how to proceed with lockdown drills, which have become as routine as fire drills as students prepare for the possibility of a shooting. Some schools opt to make the drills feel partially authentic — an approach several schools backed off from this week out of fear they would stir already heightened anxieties.

At Dysart High School in El Mirage, Ariz., the principal took extra steps to make sure students knew its previously scheduled drill on Thursday was, in fact, just a drill. The reminder was included in the morning announcements, and she reiterated it on the public address system several times throughout the day, said Zachery Fountain, a district spokesman.

Eureka High School in Eureka, Calif., postponed its drill that had been scheduled for Thursday, partly because officials were concerned about the mental state of students, said Fred Van Vleck, the district superintendent. Typically, the school doesn't announce that the lockdown is a drill, telling students only that there could be a drill within a one-week window, he said.

AS A BOY, HER GRANDFATHER SURVIVED A MASS SHOOTING BY HIDING IN A CLOSET. NOW SHE WAS DOING THE SAME.

During the horror at Stoneman Douglas High on Wednesday, Carly Novell, a 17-year-old senior who is an editor for the school's quarterly magazine, hid in a closet and thought about an awful family tragedy from before she was born. Her mother had told her about how her grandfather had survived a mass shooting in 1949 in Camden, N.J. His family had not made it.

"My grandfather was 12, and his grandma and his mom and dad were killed while he hid in a closet," Ms. Novell said. "They heard gunshots on the street, so my great-grandma told my grandpa to hide in the closet, so he was safe. But he didn't have a family after that."

Interviewed on Thursday, she said: "I was thinking of him while I was in the closet. I was wondering what he felt like while he was there. My mom has told me he was in shock after it, too — that he didn't remember how he got to the police station, or anything like that. I didn't forget anything, but I was in shock and I didn't understand what was going on."

MR. CRUZ MADE HIS FIRST COURT APPEARANCE ON THURSDAY.

In an orange jumpsuit and shackled around his hands, feet and waist, Mr. Cruz was asked if he understood the circumstances of his appearance in court. "Yes, ma'am," he whispered.

"He's sad. He's mournful," his public defender, Melisa McNeill, said afterward. "He is fully aware of what is going on, and he's just a broken human being."

Mr. Weekes, the chief assistant public defender, said lawyers were still trying to piece together the details of Mr. Cruz's life. He has a "significant" history of mental illness, according to Mr. Weekes, and may be autistic or have a learning disability. But Mr. Weekes was not ready to say whether he would pursue a mental health defense.

Howard Finkelstein, the chief public defender in Broward County, said the case would present a difficult question: Should society execute mentally ill people?

"There's no question of whether he will be convicted of capital murder 17 times," he said. "When we let one of our children fall off grid, when they are screaming for help in every way, do we have the right to kill them when we could have stopped it?"

What can the authorities do when there is a 'red flag' about mental illness?

Elected and law enforcement officials — from Mr. Trump to the Broward County sheriff — have ramped up their demands for expanded authority over the mentally ill who pose a danger. In doing so, they stepped into a long and complicated balancing act in the United States between public safety and the right to bear arms for people with mental health issues.

Others, including some gun control and mental health advocates, point to the increasing number of states that allow law enforcement officers or, in some cases, family members or others to petition a court to temporarily take guns from people who pose a danger to themselves or others.

The measures, known as 'red flag laws' or extreme risk protection orders, have shown evidence of reducing suicides in Connecticut, where the first such law was passed in 1999, and in recent years have also been passed in California, Washington and Oregon. Eighteen states, including Florida, and the District of Columbia are considering such laws this year, according to a list compiled by Everytown for Gun Safety, a nonprofit advocacy group.

Red flag laws "provide a path to remove guns from somebody in a temporary crisis," said Avery Gardiner, the co-president of the Brady Campaign to Prevent Gun Violence. And, she said, even if a family decides not to seek a gun restraining order, the fact that the option exists can prompt frank conversations with struggling relatives. Read more about the debate around mental illness and gun ownership.

AUDRA D.S. BURCH AND JULIE TURKEWITZ REPORTED FROM PARKLAND, AND PATRICIA MAZZEI FROM NEW YORK. REPORTING WAS CONTRIBUTED BY NEIL REISNER FROM PARKLAND; KATIE ROGERS FROM POMPANO BEACH, FLA.; TIMOTHY WILLIAMS, JONAH ENGEL BROMWICH, DANIEL VICTOR AND BENJAMIN MUELLER FROM NEW YORK; AND EILEEN SULLIVAN FROM WASHINGTON.

For Parents of Shooting Victims, a Support Network That Keeps Growing

BY VIVIAN YEE | FEB. 18, 2018

A CHILD IS SHOT to death. Maybe at school, maybe at the movies. It is all over TV, all over Twitter, just like the last mass shooting.

Then the cameras go away, and the parents are left in a wilderness of heartbreak. They do not know how to plan a funeral, where to get a therapist. They're not aware that scammers will try to fund-raise off their grief, that conspiracy theorists will question their tragedy, or that — hard to believe — they might, eventually, be O.K.

But lots of people do know.

"When we had this happen to us, had our daughter slaughtered, we didn't know what to do, or what was going to happen next," said Sandy Phillips, whose 24-year-old daughter, Jessica Ghawi, was one of the 12 killed in the movie theater shooting in Aurora, Colo., in 2012. "We didn't want to live. It was horrific. And nobody else understood, except other survivors."

So it is that Ms. Phillips and her husband, Lonnie Phillips, are raising money to travel to Parkland, Fla., where the Phillipses will quietly let the families of 17 of America's latest victims of mass gun violence know that they are there to listen, to advise, to hug, to cry, and, perhaps, to recruit them to the ranks of the most committed gun-control activists in the country.

The mass shootings of recent years, the proliferation of grief from rural Oregon to the tip of Florida, have forced hundreds of family members into an unwanted fellowship. Veterans like the Phillipses serve as guides in the immediate aftermath, introducing the bereaved of Sandy Hook to those of San Bernardino and the parents of Virginia Tech to those of Roseburg, in a loose but growing network.

Some mourn in private. Some confront politicians, join gun-control groups and flock to rallies. But whether they turn to advocacy or not,

Nicole Hockley, co-director of the anti-gun-violence group Sandy Hook Promise, in Florida on Friday.

many gravitate toward one another, checking on each other by Facebook or phone whenever another gunman strikes.

In a gun-control debate that often splinters along ideological lines, no one speaks more powerfully than those who survived a high-profile shooting, or the families of those who did not. The power of their testimonials goes beyond their authenticity: They, unlike politicians and advocates, can usually avoid the accusation that they are politicizing a tragedy.

Recognizing the emotional heft of such stories, groups like the Brady Campaign to Prevent Gun Violence and Everytown for Gun Safety often make themselves available to survivors and victims' families in the aftermath of mass shootings, sometimes even paying for them to travel to meet other survivors and advocates or to attend rallies, hearings and meetings with politicians. Everytown, the group founded and funded by the former New York City Mayor Michael R.

Bloomberg, runs a network of about 1,500 family members and shooting survivors who are trained in activism, including many who were affected not by mass shootings but by the smaller ones that occur daily.

They join a long tradition of families who have turned private heartbreak into public advocacy. There is Mothers Against Drunk Driving, which has successfully shifted public awareness around drunken driving and pushed for tougher laws. There is John Walsh, who became a well-known anti-crime TV personality after his son was kidnapped and killed. There are the parents of people killed by undocumented immigrants, who have seen their campaign against illegal immigration taken up by President Trump.

The difference is that mass-shooting survivors have yet to win any major victories on the federal level. So they do what they can, hoping that when the next mass shooting happens, more people will take to their cause.

"The more people that are affected in some way, the more people care; yeah, that's what it's going to take," said Jenna Yuille, whose 54-year-old mother, Cindy Yuille, was one of two people shot and killed at the Clackamas Town Center outside Portland, Ore., in December 2012. "It's horrible, but that's part of what it's going to take."

Ms. Yuille's mother died three days before the shooting at Sandy Hook Elementary School in Newtown, Conn., in which 26 people were killed, 20 of them first graders. The gun-control debate was suddenly everywhere, and Ms. Yuille, encouraged by a friend, began to speak up. She testified in support of background-check legislation in Oregon and got involved with the Everytown Survivor Network. Ms. Yuille now works for Americans for Responsible Solutions, an advocacy group founded by former Representative Gabrielle Giffords, who was shot outside an Arizona supermarket in 2011, and her husband, the retired astronaut, Capt. Mark E. Kelly.

At an Everytown training event in the spring of 2015, Ms. Yuille met Erica Lafferty, the daughter of one of the Newtown victims, Dawn Hochsprung, Sandy Hook's principal. They were around the same age; their mothers had died three days apart. The connection was instantaneous.

When they heard about the shooting at Marjory Stoneman Douglas High School on Wednesday — Ms. Yuille in a text from her boyfriend, Ms. Lafferty when she glanced at CNN — Ms. Yuille texted Ms. Lafferty to check on her.

They felt the same, they said: Tired.

"Is it bad that we're feeling so numb? Is it bad that I haven't cried?" Ms. Lafferty asked Ms. Yuille on Friday, during a joint interview. "Because I haven't."

"Same," said Ms. Yuille, 29. "I know there are other people, especially in Oregon, that see me as a leader on this issue, and being a spokesperson on this issue, so I worry about that. I don't want to let people down.

"Exactly," said Ms. Lafferty, 32, who works for Everytown. "Like, if I slow down, am I going to disappoint anyone? Am I going to disappoint myself?"

Many families, of course, do not want to be the faces of anything. They want to struggle in quiet, if not quite in peace. Some of the families of the Newtown victims have never spoken publicly about their ordeal. And some family members, Ms. Phillips said, continue to support gun rights.

Soon after the Sandy Hook shooting, Mark Mattioli, whose son James was killed at the school, testified that legislators should focus on mental health support instead of gun control. He also spoke at a National Rifle Association news conference to praise the group's school safety proposals.

But a large and growing number of families who want gun laws strengthened have chosen to seize the platform the media offers in the wake of a shooting and never to relinquish it. One man who lost his son in the Columbine High School shooting almost two decades ago, Tom Mauser, is still deeply involved in gun-control efforts in Colorado.

STEPHEN CROWLEY/THE NEW YORK TIMES

Erica Lafferty, center, whose mother was killed at Sandy Hook Elementary School, with Colin Goddard and Ann Wright of the advocacy group Everytown for Gun Safety on a lobbying trip to Washington in 2016.

"People who are affected in a personal way become lifelong dedicated volunteers to this," said Robert Bowers Disney, the vice president for organizing at the Brady Campaign. "It just fundamentally changes people's lives and experiences."

The Phillipses have been to the scene of almost every major shooting since their daughter died, usually letting local authorities and charitable organizations know that they are there if families need them. In Florida, they are planning to offer to connect the families of the teachers killed at Marjory Stoneman Douglas High School to the daughter of a teacher killed at Columbine in 1999.

"They may not be wanting to talk, but when you tell them, 'I lost my daughter in the Aurora theater massacre,' they're like, 'Oh ... my God,' " Ms. Phillips said. "It's that initial, 'Oh, you get this.'"

They offer advice on grim matters like psychological treatment (you don't need a grief counselor, they say; you need a trauma therapist) and how to fend off scammers who pretend to raise money for families, only to keep it for themselves.

Increasingly, they have had to warn people about the online trolls who will inevitably inundate them with claims that the shooting was a government hoax.

Some people take months to get in touch. Others, angry, want to talk about activism even before they bury their loved one. One man in Las Vegas who had lost his wife in the country music festival shooting knew no one else in town. So, while he waited for his wife's body to be released, he turned to Lonnie and Sandy Phillips. They are still talking.

One of the first people the Phillipses spoke to after beginning this work was Nicole Hockley, whose son, Dylan, was killed at Sandy Hook Elementary.

Ms. Hockley waited a month to meet with the Phillipses, and even then, she wondered if it was too soon. "It can also be scary to potentially see your future self from a path that you didn't choose," she said. "But also knowing that other people have survived and have found ways to keep walking forward — that can help as well."

Ms. Hockley, the co-director of the anti-gun-violence group Sandy Hook Promise, now tries to let the families of each successive wave of shooting victims know that they can lean on her for support when they are ready. She is careful to put aside her political agenda in those conversations, she said, not wanting to exploit their grief.

Ms. Hockley heard about Wednesday's Parkland shooting while on a work trip to Los Angeles. She crumbled as she learned that it was a school.

By Thursday, she was on a plane to Florida.

Scared but Resilient, Stoneman Douglas Students Return to Class

BY JACK HEALY | FEB. 28, 2018

PARKLAND, FLA. — Brooke Harrison, 14, was still in a deep sleep when her mother knocked on her door and hugged her awake at 6:45 Wednesday morning. "You need to get up," she told her daughter. "You don't want to be late for school today."

It was the first day of class for Brooke and her classmates at Marjory Stoneman Douglas High School since a mass shooting that killed 17 people and forever upended thousands of lives across this South Florida suburb two weeks ago.

It had been two weeks of nightmares, funerals, flashbacks, vigils and grief counseling since the attack. But Brooke felt ready.

She had watched gunfire explode through her Honors English class that Feb. 14 afternoon as she and her classmates worked on an essay about hardship and education. Three students from her class alone were killed. She had heard their last breaths, crawled through glass and put pressure on a wounded student's torso before escaping through the school parking lot and running as fast as she could to reach her home in a subdivision lined by coconut palms.

Now, like many other Stoneman Douglas students, Brooke just wanted to return to a routine. She wanted to see her friends and reclaim her school, which is ringed by police officers and garlanded by fading memorial flowers.

She was nervous, and she worried she would cry when she walked through the courtyard where she would sometimes eat lunch with Alaina Petty, who was killed in her classroom. Others said they dreaded confronting so many empty seats, or seeing the art project that a slain friend would never finish.

"I just hope she's going to be O.K. being there all day," Brooke's mother, Denise, said as she made coffee, toast and bacon for breakfast.

"That it's not traumatic to be there."

But first, Brooke needed her mother to help unknot a pair of gray Nikes.

"I have no strength," she said as she walked into the kitchen, smiling and still wearing the same burgundy Stoneman Douglas shirt from the day before.

The bloodied shoes that Brooke had worn the day of the shooting had been taken away as evidence. Her favorite sweater was also seized. Her black backpack now has a bullet hole in the bottom, from one of the AR-15 rifle rounds that filled her English class with a choking haze and killed Alex Schachter, Alyssa Alhadeff and Alaina before her eyes there in room 1216.

So on Wednesday, Brooke went back to school carrying little more than her phone and a small bracelet made by students that said "ALAINA."

The shortened school day started with fourth period, the class where everything had shattered. For 30 minutes, the students reunited with the classmates and teachers who had huddled with them in closets and corners. They spent 24 minutes in each of their other classes and were done by 11:40 a.m. Robert W. Runcie, the Broward schools superintendent, said about 95 percent of the student body of 3,293 had returned.

There were extra counselors and therapy dogs on hand, and it will be days — if not weeks — before students return to their regular lessons. The school's principal, Ty Thompson, said on Twitter that the focus of the week would be on healing, and classes are being dismissed at 11:40 a.m. for the rest of the week in an effort to let the students acclimate to being back.

"There is no need for backpacks," he wrote. "Come ready to start the healing process and #RECLAIM THE NEST."

Back at home that morning, it was 7:23. Time for Brooke to go.

"Are we ready?" Ms. Harrison asked.

"Yeah."

As they skimmed through the neighborhood in a white Hyundai S.U.V., past driveway basketball hoops, cyclists and joggers, Ms. Harrison remembered how she had driven the same route two weeks earlier to find Brooke after the shooting.

Many parents had exchanged frantic text messages with their children as they hid in their classrooms, but Brooke's class was one of the first to be attacked. When she and her friends poured out of the school, they grabbed cellphones from strangers and broke the news to their parents. Brooke's mother found her shaken near their subdivision.

That day, Brooke and two friends had sat at her house and feverishly tried to confirm which of their friends was safe. They sent group text messages asking who was missing and who had been found. They posted photos on social media. They knew, before any names were officially released or parents were notified, which of their friends were not coming home.

Brooke still flashes back to the shadow of the gunman passing by their classroom door. "I'll just see him," she said. These past two weeks, she found some escape in a high school romance novel and rewatched "101 Dalmatians" and other Disney movies from her childhood.

Her parents tried to calibrate when to hold her close and when to give her space. Ms. Harrison said she would quietly try to check in by calling Brooke to ask if she wanted a drink from Starbucks or needed anything from Target. And when Brooke declined to attend her 12-year-old brother's birthday party, she reminded her mother that she sometimes just needed to be alone.

On Wednesday, traffic around the school slowed to a crawl as Brooke and her mother drew close. They passed heavily armed police officers and television cameras. Students walked through a colonnade of police officers from nearby cities and teachers from their old middle and elementary schools who waved signs of support.

"Welcome back, welcome back," one sheriff's deputy said.

"I feel like I'm on an episode of 'C.S.I.,'" Brooke said.

"How is this our school?" her mother asked. "How is this happening?"

Ms. Harrison's voice trembled. "This is unbelievable. It's making me sad."

"Mom, please don't cry."

They pulled into a circular driveway, near a banner that declared "WELCOME EAGLES" — their school team name. Inside, over the course of this half-day, there would be hugs and joyful reunions laced with sadness and loss. Some students would break down crying as they said the Pledge of Allegiance. Others would wipe away tears when they heard the alma mater. They would compare their memories, nuzzle therapy dogs and share their final text messages from now-absent friends.

"We were just so happy to see each other," Brooke would say.

But not quite yet. Brooke and her mother quickly hugged, kissed and said I love you. And then the 14-year-old freshman who dreams about one day whirling across the globe as a travel journalist hopped out of her mom's car, threaded her way past a sheriff's officer and joined the river of children in burgundy T-shirts making their way back in.

My Teachers at Marjory Stoneman Douglas Saved Lives

OPINION | BY CARSON ABT | FEB. 26, 2018

PARKLAND, FLA. — As a student at Marjory Stoneman Douglas High School, it's hard for me to believe that the school on TV is mine. No one believes a school shooting will happen to them until they are scrambling to find their friends and family. In the end, 17 families were not able to find their loved ones.

As Albus Dumbledore, the wise headmaster of Harry Potter's Hogwarts, said, "Happiness can be found in the darkest of times, if one only remembers to turn on the light." My teachers are the light. Through a combination of training and determination, they calmed the fear of some and saved the lives of others. When schools across the country lower their flags and share our darkness, they should also share our light. Maybe heroism can't be taught, but preparedness certainly can be. Every teacher should have training for a school shooting like mine did.

On Wednesday, I took that message to President Trump at his White House listening session with students and parents from Parkland. The next day, he announced his disapproval of my idea that schools should have more active shooter training. If I had known he felt this way, I would have told him my story.

Fifteen minutes before the dismissal bell, the fire alarm rang and my class was evacuated after an administrator came on the intercom and gave the order. By the time the administrator made the announcement to take shelter in classrooms, we were too far away to turn back. So we kept going. The entire time, teachers were calling for their students to stay close as they tried to count them all. The teachers were calm, so the students tried to stay calm too. My teacher for that class, Ms. Hitchcock, told us to keep walking. It was reassuring when she took attendance and the entire class was present. Ms. Hitchcock provided order in a moment of chaos. I knew at least some of my friends were safe.

Our school regularly has fire drills (as we did the morning of the shooting), tornado drills and lockdown drills. Just six weeks ago, my teachers did a training session on active shooter situations, known as Code Red. All doors must be locked, lights are turned off and students are kept in the classrooms away from windows. For any type of emergency or drill, teachers must account for all their students. After the training, the teachers discussed with the students in each of their classes what to do. We were told where to hide and how to evacuate.

Not every school has the training we do. Eighteen states do not require their school districts to develop emergency plans, according to the Government Accountability Office. In the rest, 59 percent of districts reported difficulty balancing emergency planning with other priorities. There is no priority higher than saving lives.

My teachers' training saved lives. Teachers frantically yelled for their students to go back into classrooms, saving some who were unknowingly running toward the shooter.

Mr. Gard, my math teacher two years ago, evacuated his classroom due to the fire alarm that went off just before the shooting started. But he immediately pulled the students back into his classroom closet when the Code Red was declared. He turned off the lights, locked his classroom door and counted his students. Mr. Gard knew what to do and he saved lives as a result.

At the sound of gunshots, one of my teachers last year, Mr. Rospierski, hurried students into locked classrooms, a protocol reinforced in the teacher training sessions. Then he stayed in the hallway to guide eight stranded students away from the shooter, who was in that same hallway.

My high school is not the only one to benefit from training for a situation like this. Three months ago, an elementary school in Northern California blocked a shooter from entering classrooms using similar protocols and saving countless lives. Every district can make itself safer through similar training.

Active-shooter training is not the panacea to end school shootings. But it is an essential part of keeping schools safe. Whether one supports arming teachers, an assault weapons ban, or any other measure to reduce gun violence, everyone should see that active-shooter training should be part of a program to address school shootings.

President Trump is hosting governors from all 50 states to discuss school safety. I urge him to talk to Gov. Rick Scott of Florida, who has proposed increasing the amount of training and drills for active shooter scenarios. I ask him to think about my story. I ask him to reconsider his position on this issue.

CARSON ABT IS A JUNIOR AT MARJORY STONEMAN DOUGLAS HIGH SCHOOL.

In School Shooting's Painful Aftermath, Sheriff Faces Questions Over Police Response

BY ALAN BLINDER, PATRICIA MAZZEI AND RICHARD A. OPPEL JR. | FEB. 21, 2018

CORAL SPRINGS, FLA. — The Broward County sheriff on Wednesday defended his office's response to one of the deadliest school shootings in American history amid questions over whether some of his deputies hung back instead of pursuing the gunman accused of killing 17 people.

Sheriff Scott Israel said that, to his knowledge, deputies followed protocol and did not wait for specialized teams to arrive before going into Marjory Stoneman Douglas High School in Parkland, Fla. But he said that details over the office's response remained unclear.

"That's exactly what we're examining," Sheriff Israel said, noting that active shooter protocols require confronting suspects as quickly as possible. "You don't wait for SWAT, you get in, and you push toward the shooter."

The sheriff's response comes a week after Nikolas Cruz was accused of opening fire at his former school with a semiautomatic AR-15 rifle and as parents, students and school administrators continue to struggle to make sense of what happened.

After the attack, Mr. Cruz slipped away on foot seven minutes after the gunfire began and was ultimately stopped by an officer from a neighboring police department.

Sheriff Israel also said that the only armed guard at Stoneman Douglas High, Deputy Scot Peterson, never discharged his gun during the shooting.

"The response and actions of Deputy Peterson will be looked at and scrutinized, as will everyone's," Sheriff Israel said, adding that trained deputies would begin carrying rifles on school grounds.

Interviews with law enforcement officers, parents and students, as well as a review of police radio traffic immediately after the shooting, make clear the widespread confusion among the authorities.

Many emergency medical workers had no idea where the suspect was for at least 30 minutes after the gunfire erupted, and the authorities struggled to identify him for another 15 minutes. All the while, rescue workers tended to victims under the cover of officers with long rifles, some of whom appear to have entered the school less than 10 minutes after the gunfire began — but just after the suspect fled.

For as long as 45 minutes after the shooting stopped, some students were still cowering behind locked doors, unsure if the person banging on their door was a police officer or the gunman, according to students.

By the time Avril Engelhart, a 15-year-old freshman, heard the police enter the freshman building, where she was hiding inside her English classroom, maybe 10 minutes had passed since the gunman began firing, she said.

"He wasn't really shooting anymore," she said. "We could hear them outside our door, and on the police walkie-talkie, we heard them say, 'We have a victim down.' And people started crying."

To be sure, mass shootings are always chaotic and, despite the best efforts of trained police officers and emergency medical workers, the authorities often struggle with figuring out how to stop a gunman set on inflicting grievous harm in a matter of minutes.

"They're all pretty much the same in that it's over in three to five minutes," said Al Lamberti, Sheriff Israel's predecessor, referring to the Columbine and Sandy Hook shootings. "We have to learn from this, just like we did from the others."

For parents and students, the whereabouts of the campus deputy has remained a troubling question. Sheriff Israel reiterated that Deputy Peterson was elsewhere on campus, but would not say where.

A second deputy, assigned to Westglades Middle School adjacent to the high school, was away on training last Wednesday, a spokeswoman for the sheriff's office said.

"Where was the only guy with a gun when this happened?" asked Karen Dietrich, a Fort Lauderdale police officer whose two sons attend Stoneman Douglas High and survived the massacre. "I realize it's a large campus, and he may have been on the other side, I don't know. But it would not take six minutes on a full run to get from one end to the other."

Tim Burton, a Coral Springs police officer assigned to a nearby elementary school, responded to the shooting. He said in an interview on Wednesday that he had seen Deputy Peterson in a Stoneman Douglas High parking lot, where at least one school employee believed the gunman might be.

Deputy Peterson "was seeking cover behind a concrete column leading to a stairwell," said Officer Burton, who worried the gunman could be lurking in the lot because he heard no gunshots or screams to guide him toward the site of the shooting.

Deputy Peterson, who has been in law enforcement for more than 30 years, could not be reached for comment, and no one answered the door at his home in neighboring Palm Beach County. The Broward Sheriff's Office Deputies Association, a labor union, said Deputy Peterson has not sought representation from the association since the shooting. He remains on active duty, a spokeswoman for the sheriff's office said.

Sheriff Israel, who immediately after the shooting praised his department's response, abruptly called a news conference on Wednesday to extend plaudits to other police departments, including Coral Springs, whose officers said they were the first to arrive at the high school, which is in the neighboring city of Parkland

"I don't know what deputies or police officers went in first, or in what order they arrived," Sheriff Israel said. "This is a fluid investigation."

Among the first to respond was Sgt. Jeff Heinrich, an off-duty Coral Springs police officer who was doing maintenance work on the baseball field when he heard gunfire. He saw students running, heard screams and got to work, treating a boy with a gunshot wound. He eventually grabbed a fellow officer's extra weapon, slipped on a bullet-resistant vest and started searching the school, where his wife teaches physical education and his son is in the 11th grade.

"When those shots ring out, you have a job to do," Sergeant Heinrich said in an interview on Wednesday. "Everybody's instinct is to go the other way. You have to fight that instinct."

The shooting at Columbine High School in 1999 fundamentally changed police protocol amid fears that a gunman or gunmen equipped with semiautomatic weapons would be capable of killing dozens of people in a matter of moments. Officers, their patrol cars now stocked with supplies like rifles, ballistic helmets and trauma care kits, are now trained to seek gunmen urgently, even if they have no backup or only limited information.

Sheriff Israel, however, noted in a local television interview on Wednesday that he learned after the Fort Lauderdale airport shooting, in January 2017, that it was not always helpful for deputies to rush into an active scene.

"One of the key lessons we learned from the airport was the phenomenon of self-dispatching and not allowing deputies and police officers from all over the tri-county area to just arrive haphazardly," he told the local CBS affiliate. "People who came went to a staging area, and they were inserted into the mission in a common-sense way, and everybody had a job to do."

Not a single law enforcement officer appears to have fired their gun inside Stoneman Douglas High — an indication of how little the police could do once the suspect had fled after firing more than 100 rounds down the hallways and into four classrooms on two floors of the freshman building. The authorities said he had enough time to make it to the third floor to take off a tactical vest and drop off his weapon and high-capacity magazines in a stairwell.

"There were a lot of kids screaming, officers just trying to get into doorways, trying to find not only the bad guy, but grab victims, trying to reach victims, pull them out and get them to fire-rescue as quickly as possible for transport," recalled Sgt. Carla Kmiotek of Coral Springs, who oversees training for her department and was one of the first officers to enter the building.

As she searched the high school, she said, "I had a talk with myself, accepting that I could end up getting killed in this incident."

Sergeant Heinrich, who in 2016 arrested an armed boy at nearby Coral Springs High School, said his response to the shooting had felt automated.

"This is go-time," he said. "This is what we train for. This is what we do."

The teenager Sergeant Heinrich had begun to treat survived the shooting, but remains hospitalized. The sergeant is planning to visit on Thursday for his first meeting with him since their encounter at the school. When he goes, he will be returning the teenager's backpack, which had been lost in the chaos.

The Things We Know About School Shooters

OPINION | BY ERICA GOODE | FEB. 15, 2018

FIVE YEARS AGO, shortly after the elementary school massacre in Newtown, Conn., I visited a program in Los Angeles aimed at heading off school shootings before they occurred.

What I learned was both terrifying and encouraging. High schools and colleges, it turned out, were rife with troubled students who expressed violent thoughts. One scribbled "Kill Everyone Leave None Alive" in a notebook beside drawings of bombs hitting a building that looked disturbingly like a school. Another posted pictures of himself on Facebook holding guns alongside the words "School — Tomorrow." A third student said that Adam Lanza, the Newtown shooter, had done a good thing in killing those 20 children by enabling them to escape the travails of life.

But I also realized that mental health experts, law enforcement agencies and criminal justice researchers had learned a great deal about how to identify potential perpetrators of school violence, how to assess whether the threats were real — a vast majority are not — and how to intervene. With at least 17 people dead at a high school in Parkland, Fla., on Wednesday and 40 school shootings recorded in the United States since 2000, it is worth paying attention to what this knowledge is.

Studies have shown, for example, that in school shootings, the killers virtually always "leak" their intentions, leaving a trail of clues behind them. Nikolas Cruz, the 19-year-old who the police said has confessed in the Parkland shooting, apparently was no exception: Students reportedly avoided him and joked that if anyone were going to shoot up the school, it would be him.

Researchers have also found that in many, if not most, cases of school violence, the perpetrator has done extensive research on previ-

ous school shootings, studying them in detail, often with special attention to the killings at Columbine High School in 1999. A study of nine
school shootings in Europe conducted by J. Reid Meloy, a forensic psychologist in San Diego who consults on threat assessment for schools
and corporations, found that a third of the killers had "consciously imi-
tated and emulated what had happened in Columbine."

Finally, there is nascent, but increasing, evidence that violence
begets violence, with one school shooting — especially if it receives
a lot of publicity — leading to others, a phenomenon that researchers
refer to as "contagion." And some psychologists believe that news
media reports of mass killings may propel people who are already at
risk of violence into committing copycat crimes.

Violence is, of course, notoriously difficult to predict, and no one
thinks that all school shootings can be prevented. Yet experts in
assessing threats say that there are approaches that in some cases
can be effective in derailing a planned act of violence.

Improved communication among agencies authorized to detect
and prevent violence is one promising strategy. In many areas where
there are coordinated threat assessment systems in place, barriers to
such communication have been dismantled to reduce the chances that
a student who is "on a path to violence" will fall through the cracks.

But few localities have as comprehensive a system as I saw in Los
Angeles County, where law enforcement, the county mental health
department and educational institutions share information and train
staff members to recognize and report worrisome behavior. Students,
teachers and parents are encouraged to report any troubling behavior.
When a threat appears potentially serious, mental health workers and
law enforcement officers might visit a student's home, talk to the parents and even ask if they can see the student's room.

Tony Beliz, a consultant to schools and corporations on violence
prevention who for many years ran the mental health side of the
Los Angeles program, which was started by the Los Angeles Police
Department, has noted that parents often have no idea what their

children are up to. In more than a few cases, a team visiting a home has found weapons or other indications of deadly intention.

School shootings are rare events, and account for only a tiny fraction of gun-related deaths each year. Still, many experts believe that it should be far more difficult for severely troubled teenagers to get hold of weapons like the semiautomatic AR-15 used in the Parkland, Fla., attack. In California, disturbed teenagers who seem seriously bent on violence can sometimes be committed to a psychiatric hospital for 72 hours of observation, an action that then allows any firearms they possess to be legally seized. In other states, it is not so easy.

Educating local clinics, school psychologists and teachers about laws governing the release of privileged communication can improve the chances of identifying potentially dangerous students. Many educators and mental health professionals believe that they cannot disclose troubling confidences, even if they believe that there might be a threat to public safety. But this is not the case.

Dr. Meloy, the forensic psychologist, and other experts think the media can also do more to prevent mass shootings. He does not expect news outlets to forgo covering school shootings. But, Dr. Meloy says, reporters and editors could avoid describing a killer using words that might "convey a certain cool pose" to some teenagers, including "lone wolf" or even "school shooter."

"From the perspective of a young male, being a school shooter is something that can be idealized, and it brings a coolness to the behavior that otherwise does not exist in his life," Dr. Meloy told me.

After my trip five years ago, I wrote a story about the Los Angeles program and others like it and left feeling hopeful that even if our society can't stop school shootings altogether, we can certainly reduce their frequency.

The horrific shooting in Parkland raises the question of whether we are serious about trying.

ERICA GOODE, A FORMER NEW YORK TIMES REPORTER, IS A VISITING PROFESSOR AT THE S.I. NEWHOUSE SCHOOL OF PUBLIC COMMUNICATIONS.

Tipster's Warning to F.B.I. on Florida Shooting Suspect: 'I Know He's Going to Explode'

BY RICHARD A. OPPEL JR., SERGE F. KOVALESKI, PATRICIA MAZZEI AND
ADAM GOLDMAN | FEB. 23, 2018

THE WARNINGS that law enforcement officials received about Nikolas Cruz were anything but subtle.

"I know he's going to explode," a woman who knew Mr. Cruz said on the F.B.I.'s tip line on Jan. 5. Her big worry was that he might resort to slipping "into a school and just shooting the place up." Forty days later, Mr. Cruz is accused of doing just that, barging into his former high school in Parkland, Fla., and shooting 17 people to death.

Three months before the Feb. 14 massacre at Marjory Stoneman Douglas High School, a family friend dialed 911 to tell the Palm Beach County sheriff's office about Mr. Cruz's personal arsenal. "I need someone here because I'm afraid he comes back and he has a lot of weapons," the friend said.

Mr. Cruz, 19, himself called the authorities just after Thanksgiving, describing how he had been in a fight and was struggling with the death of his mother. "The thing is I lost my mother a couple of weeks ago, so like I am dealing with a bunch of things right now," he said in a childlike voice, sounding agitated and out of breath.

The authorities have acknowledged mishandling numerous warning signs that Mr. Cruz was deeply troubled. There were tips to the F.B.I. about disturbing social media posts. There were visits by social services to his home. There were dozens of calls to 911 and the local authorities, some mentioning fears that he was capable of violence.

Reviewing the transcripts of those calls, and listening to the audio-tapes of some of them, is a chilling exercise that makes Mr. Cruz's arrest in one of America's deadliest school shootings seem less than a complete surprise.

In a 911 call on Nov. 29, Rocxanne Deschamps, the family friend who took in Mr. Cruz after the death of his mother, expressed fear that he was going to get a gun after fighting with her son. Ms. Deschamps lives in a faded, off-white mobile home, where Mr. Cruz and his younger brother, Zachary, stayed with her briefly.

In Ms. Deschamps's 911 call, she told the dispatcher that Mr. Cruz already had about eight guns that he kept at a friend's house and that he had just been thrown out of the house after the tantrum in which he punched the walls, hurled things around her home and got into a fight with Rock, her 22-year-old son.

"He got pissed off and then he came in the house and started banging all the doors and banging in the walls and hitting the walls and throwing everything in the room," she said. "And then my son got in there and he said, 'Stop it,' and he didn't want to stop."

She added: "It's not the first time he put a gun on somebody's head." Ms. Deschamps made it clear that her new houseguest was obsessed with firearms and had threatened both his mother and his brother. "That's all he wants is his gun," she said. "And that's all he cares about is his gun. He bought tons of bullets and stuff and I took it away from him."

Ms. Deschamps declined to comment on Friday, and her lawyer did not respond to phone messages and emails over the past week.

More than once, Mr. Cruz was identified by those around him as someone capable of carrying out a school shooting

On Nov. 30, two and a half months before the Parkland massacre, an unidentified caller from Massachusetts told the Broward County Sheriff's Office that Mr. Cruz was collecting guns and knives and that "he could be a school shooter in the making."

Two years before, the office reported receiving "thirdhand information" from the son of one of Mr. Cruz's neighbors that he "planned to shoot up the school on Instagram."

The tip that the F.B.I. received in early January from someone close to Mr. Cruz suggested that he owned a gun and had talked about carrying out a school shooting. But the bureau failed to investigate, even though the tipster said Mr. Cruz had a "desire to kill people, erratic behavior and disturbing social media posts."

That information should have been sent to the Miami F.B.I. field office, the bureau said.

The F.B.I. also received a tip from a bail bondsman in Mississippi in September about a suspicious comment left on his YouTube channel by a "nikolas cruz" who professed a desire to be a "professional school shooter." The bondsman notified YouTube, which promptly took down the comment.

The F.B.I. said it did not have enough information to determine if "nikolas cruz" was a real name or a pseudonym, and the bureau said it could not justify keeping a file on the tip open and closed it in October.

When the second tip reached the F.B.I. in West Virginia in January, a specialist was able to view the earlier tip, too. But even then, the specialist, in consultation with her supervisor, decided that there was not enough evidence to pursue it and that it did not appear to be an imminent threat.

The acting F.B.I. deputy director, David L. Bowdich, briefed congressional staff members about the case on Friday and acknowledged the bureau's failure to investigate, according to three people with direct knowledge of the meeting.

Over the course of the January call, which lasted more than 13 minutes, the tipster warned the F.B.I. that Mr. Cruz had been adrift since his mother's death in November. She said that Mr. Cruz had "the mental capacity of a 12 to a 14 year old." The tipster provided four Instagram accounts for Mr. Cruz, which she said showed photos of sliced up animals and the firearms he had amassed. The caller, whose name was redacted on the transcript, said Mr. Cruz had used money from his mother's account after her death to purchase the weapons.

"If you go onto his Instagram pages, you'll see all the guns," the woman said.

Before calling the F.B.I., the woman telephoned Broward sheriff's deputies in Parkland, worried that Mr. Cruz might kill himself. But she did not hear back from them and became increasingly alarmed after she said Mr. Cruz posted online that "he wants to kill people."

Two deputies have been placed on restricted duty while the Broward office investigates how two calls about Mr. Cruz — the one in November and an earlier one in 2016 — may have been mishandled.

Before she died in early November, Mr. Cruz's mother, Lynda Cruz, had called the authorities numerous times over the past decade to report her son. She said he had hit her with the plastic hose from a vacuum, and once threw her against the wall after she took his Xbox away, adding that he suffered from anger issues as well as attention deficit hyperactivity disorder and obsessive-compulsive disorder.

Mr. Cruz progressed to more distressing behavior, including possibly shooting a neighbor's chicken with a BB gun, collecting hate symbols, cutting himself, and possibly swallowing gasoline in a failed suicide attempt, according to complaints to the local authorities.

The Boys Are Not All Right

OPINION | BY MICHAEL IAN BLACK | FEB. 21, 2018

I USED TO HAVE this one-liner: "If you want to emasculate a guy friend, when you're at a restaurant, ask him everything that he's going to order, and then when the waitress comes … order for him." It's funny because it shouldn't be that easy to rob a man of his masculinity — but it is.

Last week, 17 people, most of them teenagers, were shot dead at a Florida school. Marjory Stoneman Douglas High School now joins the ranks of Sandy Hook, Virginia Tech, Columbine and too many other sites of American carnage. What do these shootings have in common? Guns, yes. But also, boys. Girls aren't pulling the triggers. It's boys. It's almost always boys.

America's boys are broken. And it's killing us.

The brokenness of the country's boys stands in contrast to its girls, who still face an abundance of obstacles but go into the world increasingly well equipped to take them on.

The past 50 years have redefined what it means to be female in America. Girls today are told that they can do anything, be anyone. They've absorbed the message: They're outperforming boys in school at every level. But it isn't just about performance. To be a girl today is to be the beneficiary of decades of conversation about the complexities of womanhood, its many forms and expressions.

Boys, though, have been left behind. No commensurate movement has emerged to help them navigate toward a full expression of their gender. It's no longer enough to "be a man" — we no longer even know what that means.

Too many boys are trapped in the same suffocating, outdated model of masculinity, where manhood is measured in strength, where there is no way to be vulnerable without being emasculated, where manliness is about having power over others. They are trapped, and they don't even have the language to talk about how they feel about being trapped, because the language that exists to discuss the full range of human emotion is still viewed as sensitive and feminine.

Men feel isolated, confused and conflicted about their natures. Many feel that the very qualities that used to define them — their strength, aggression and competitiveness — are no longer wanted or needed; many others never felt strong or aggressive or competitive to begin with. We don't know how to be, and we're terrified.

But to even admit our terror is to be reduced, because we don't have a model of masculinity that allows for fear or grief or tenderness or the day-to-day sadness that sometimes overtakes us all.

Case in point: A few days ago, I posted a brief thread about these thoughts on Twitter, knowing I would receive hateful replies in response. I got dozens of messages impugning my manhood; the mildest of them called me a "soy boy" (a common insult among the alt-right that links soy intake to estrogen).

And so the man who feels lost but wishes to preserve his fully masculine self has only two choices: withdrawal or rage. We've seen what withdrawal and rage have the potential to do. School shootings are only the most public of tragedies. Others, on a smaller scale, take place across the country daily; another commonality among shooters is a history of abuse toward women.

To be clear, most men will never turn violent. Most men will turn out fine. Most will learn to navigate the deep waters of their feelings without ever engaging in any form of destruction. Most will grow up to be kind. But many will not.

We will probably never understand why any one young man decides to end the lives of others. But we can see at least one pattern and that pattern is glaringly obvious. It's boys.

I believe in boys. I believe in my son. Sometimes, though, I see him, 16 years old, swallowing his frustration, burying his worry, stomping up the stairs without telling us what's wrong, and I want to show him what it looks like to be vulnerable and open but I can't. Because I was a boy once, too.

There has to be a way to expand what it means to be a man without losing our masculinity. I don't know how we open ourselves to the rich complexity of our manhood. I think we would benefit from the same conversations girls and women have been having for these past 50 years.

I would like men to use feminism as an inspiration, in the same way that feminists used the civil rights movement as theirs. I'm not advocating a quick fix. There isn't one. But we have to start the conversation. Boys are broken, and I want to help.

MICHAEL IAN BLACK (@MICHAELIANBLACK) IS A COMEDIAN, ACTOR AND AUTHOR.

N.R.A. Chief, Wayne LaPierre, Offers Fierce Defense of 2nd Amendment

BY JEREMY W. PETERS | FEB. 22, 2018

OXON HILL, MD. — The head of the National Rifle Association, Wayne LaPierre, leveled a searing indictment on Thursday against liberal Democrats, the news media and political opportunists he said were joined together in a socialist plot to "eradicate all individual freedoms."

Mr. LaPierre's remarks, his first since a gunman took the lives of 17 people at a Florida high school last week, seemed aimed at blunting the rising public pressure for stricter gun control. Conservatives, he said, needed to push back even as liberals tried to smear them.

"The shameful politicization of tragedy — it's a classic strategy, right out of the playbook of a poisonous movement," he said to a friendly but largely restrained crowd at the annual Conservative Political Action Conference. "They hate the N.R.A. They hate the Second Amendment. They hate individual freedom."

The solution Mr. LaPierre offered was not to pass new laws but to better enforce the existing background check system and, he said, "harden our schools" with more armed guards.

"Evil walks among us," he added, making a passing reference to "another terrible tragedy" in the Parkland, Fla., school massacre.

Mr. LaPierre's pugnacious appearance appeared to signal a tactical shift for the N.R.A., which had officially remained mostly quiet in the week after the Florida shooting, even as a movement of young people, including survivors of the massacre, made emotional pleas for gun control. The organization typically uses the first few days after an episode of mass gun violence to lie low before it comes out hard in opposition to any new gun control measures.

"The N.R.A. will not only speak out," he said, "we will speak out louder and we will speak out stronger than ever before."

Mr. LaPierre, who for around three decades has been the N.R.A.'s public face of unwavering resistance to tighter restrictions on guns, used his speech to play to the fear and mistrust that many on the right have toward government.

He raised the specter of mass gun confiscation. He accused federal agencies like the Justice Department of weaponizing their power to punish political enemies. He warned darkly that "our country will be changed forever" at the hands of socialist conspirators.

"History proves it. Every time in every nation in which this political disease rises to power, its citizens are repressed, their freedoms are destroyed and their firearms are banned and confiscated," he said, reading slowly and deliberately from his prepared text.

Mr. LaPierre's appearance each year at the conference, known as CPAC, is typically an event that passes without much notice. But this year, coming just a week after one of the worst school shootings in American history, CPAC seemed to take on the feel of an N.R.A. forum.

Mr. LaPierre's name was initially left off the program. Then, on Thursday morning, the conference's organizers released a revised schedule with both Mr. LaPierre and Dana Loesch, an N.R.A. spokeswoman, added as speakers.

Outside the hall where they spoke, an N.R.A. booth was broadcasting hours of online video programming from its in-house news channel, NRATV, which the organization has used as an early-warning system to alert its followers to gun control efforts.

Ms. Loesch, who just hours earlier had appeared subdued as she spoke softly in defense of the N.R.A. at a contentious forum in Florida hosted by CNN, reverted to the caustic, insult-lobbing persona she has cultivated on NRATV, where she is also a host.

Speaking before Mr. LaPierre, she called for more guns in schools, denounced the Justice Department and the Federal Bureau of Investigation as political persecutors and accused liberals of trying to sabotage the existing background check system for gun purchases.

Ms. Loesch also blamed James B. Comey, the F.B.I. director fired by President Trump amid a dispute over the bureau's investigation of possible ties between the Trump campaign and Russians, for indirectly causing the Parkland massacre.

"Maybe if you politicized your agency less and did your job more, we wouldn't have these problems," she sneered.

Ms. Loesch also saw fault for the shooting in the news media, saying killings were always good for business. "Many in legacy media love mass shootings," she said. "Crying white mothers are ratings gold to you and many in the legacy media in the back."

But the temperature on stage was noticeably hotter than in the audience, which gave Mr. LaPierre and Ms. Loesch polite but mostly unenthusiastic applause.

Mr. LaPierre evidently noticed, prompting him to comment on the stillness in the hall, which he wrote off as fear over the government oppression he warned was coming. "I hear a lot of quiet in this room," he said. "I sense your anxiety. And you should be anxious. You should be frightened."

He repeatedly returned to his attacks against gun control advocates as socialists lying in wait.

"And oh how socialists love to make lists," he said, "especially lists that can be used to deny citizens their basic freedoms."

The Florida school shooting hung over many of the day's speeches at CPAC. And with only small exceptions — like when Betsy DeVos, the education secretary, asked for a moment of silence for the victims — speakers directed blame and scorn on the news media.

Ben Shapiro, a conservative podcast host and author, called on reporters to stop showing the faces and printing the names of school shooters, as he said his website had done.

Senator Ted Cruz of Texas said he found much of the news media coverage, including the emotional outpouring at a CNN forum on Wednesday, "tiresome."

"Every time you see a horrific crime, people in the media and Democratic politicians immediately try to leap on it to advance their agenda," Mr. Cruz said. "And their agenda is stripping away Second Amendment rights away from law-abiding citizens."

He noted what he said was one of the biggest moments for applause at the CNN event: "It was about confiscating guns."

Florida Legislator's Aide Is Fired After He Calls Parkland Students 'Actors'

BY MAGGIE ASTOR | FEB. 20, 2018

AN AIDE to State Representative Shawn Harrison of Florida was fired on Tuesday after claiming falsely that two students at Marjory Stoneman Douglas High School were "actors that travel to various crisis when they happen," a common far-right conspiracy theory after mass shootings.

Mr. Harrison's district secretary, Benjamin Kelly, made the assertion in an email sent from his state account to a Tampa Bay Times reporter, Alex Leary. Mr. Leary, who posted a screen shot of the email on Twitter, had written about far-right attacks on the students fighting for new gun laws in response to the shooting at their school last week, which killed 17 people.

Mr. Kelly's email referred to Emma González, 18, and David Hogg, 17, two seniors who have been outspoken in the days since the shooting. The Broward County superintendent, Robert W. Runcie, confirmed to The Tampa Bay Times that they were Stoneman Douglas students.

Richard Corcoran, the speaker of the Florida House, announced Tuesday evening that he had fired Mr. Kelly at Mr. Harrison's request. Mr. Harrison confirmed the firing in his own statement on Twitter, shortly after voting against consideration of a bill that would have banned assault rifles like the one used in the Stoneman Douglas shooting. (A motion to take up debate on the bill failed, 36 to 71, on a party-line vote.)

"I am appalled at and strongly denounce his comments about the Parkland students," Mr. Harrison, a Republican representing a district north of Tampa, tweeted, adding that Mr. Kelly had made his remarks "without my knowledge." Mr. Harrison did not immediately respond to a voice mail message at his Tallahassee office, and the voice mail at his district office was full.

In a tweet confirming his firing, Mr. Kelly said that he had "made a mistake whereas I tried to inform a reporter of information relating to his story regarding a school shooting," and that Mr. Harrison should not "be held responsible for my error in judgement."

Mr. Kelly did not respond to a Twitter message asking whether he stood by his claim that the students were actors, and whether his "error in judgment" was in believing that or simply in sharing the belief with a reporter. By 8:30 p.m. on Tuesday, he had made all his tweets private.

Earlier in the day, as students boarded a bus to lobby state lawmakers in Tallahassee, Cameron Kasky, a 17-year-old junior at Stoneman Douglas, urged his classmates not to let conspiracy theories distract them.

"Over the next couple days, there are a lot of people who are being paid a lot of money to ruin what we are doing," Mr. Kasky said. "A lot of the people with cameras here are here to help, and a lot of the people with cameras here are here to destroy us."

"Everybody," he added, "do not let people try to get under your skin. Do not let the disgusting side of the incredibly helpful media hurt you. Do not let these people exploit you. All they want is for you to say something to bring us down so they can shoot more of us."

JULIE TURKEWITZ CONTRIBUTED REPORTING.

Trump Finds Unlikely Culprit in School Shootings: Obama Discipline Policies

BY ERICA L. GREEN | MARCH 13, 2018

WASHINGTON — After a gunman marauded through Marjory Stoneman Douglas High School last month, conservative commentators — looking for a culprit — seized on an unlikely target: an Obama-era guidance document that sought to rein in the suspensions and expulsions of minority students.

Black students have never been the perpetrators of the mass shootings that have shocked the nation's conscience nor have minority schools been the targets. But the argument went that any relaxation of disciplinary efforts could let a killer slip through the cracks.

And this week, President Trump made the connection, announcing that Education Secretary Betsy DeVos will lead a school safety commission charged in part with examining the "repeal of the Obama administration's 'Rethink School Discipline' policies."

To civil rights groups, connecting an action to help minority students with mass killings in suburban schools smacked of burdening black children with a largely white scourge.

"Yet again, the Trump administration, faced with a domestic crisis, has responded by creating a commission to study an unrelated issue in order to ultimately advance a discriminatory and partisan goal," said Sherrilyn Ifill, the president and director-counsel at NAACP Legal Defense and Educational Fund Inc.

"School shootings are a grave and preventable problem, but rescinding the school discipline guidance is not the answer," she said. "Repealing the guidance will not stop the next school shooter, but it will ensure that thousands more students of color are unnecessarily ushered into the school-to-prison pipeline."

The issue of the Obama-era discipline guidance was raised formally by Senator Marco Rubio, Republican of Florida, who, after seeing a flurry of conservative news media reports, wrote a letter to Ms. DeVos and Attorney General Jeff Sessions questioning whether the guidance allowed the shooting suspect, Nikolas Cruz, to evade law enforcement and carry out the massacre at Stoneman Douglas High.

It was, on its face, an odd point: Mr. Cruz is white, and far from evading school disciplinary procedures, he had been expelled from Stoneman Douglas.

"The overarching goals of the 2014 directive to mitigate the school-to-prison pipeline, reduce suspensions and expulsions, and to prevent racially biased discipline are laudable and should be explored," Mr. Rubio wrote, asking that the guidance be revised. "However, any policy seeking to achieve these goals requires basic common sense and an understanding that failure to report troubled students, like Cruz, to law enforcement can have dangerous repercussions."

SAUL MARTINEZ FOR THE NEW YORK TIMES

Students leaving Marjory Stoneman Douglas High School in Parkland, Fla., after last month's shooting. The suspect, Nikolas Cruz, is white, and far from evading disciplinary procedures, he had been expelled from the school.

Broward County educators and advocates saw Mr. Rubio's letter as an indictment of a program called Promise, which the county instituted in 2013 — one year before the Obama guidance was issued — and has guided its discipline reforms to reduce student-based arrests in Broward County, where Stoneman Douglas is.

The N.A.A.C.P. said that Mr. Rubio "notably backs away from raising the purchase age for assault-style rifles and restricting magazine capacity," and instead focuses on a system that once sent one million minority students to Florida jails for "simple and routine discipline issues ranging from talking back to teachers to schoolyard scuffles."

The program was praised by former Secretary of Education Arne Duncan, and echoes the goals of the 2014 Obama guidance in discouraging schools from using law enforcement as a first line of defense for low-level offenses.

In the days before making his request, Mr. Rubio released a proposal that he said would remedy lapses in the Promise program and the 2014 guidance.

In a tweet on Tuesday, Mr. Rubio noted that the gunman was not in the Promise program, but had displayed violent and threatening behavior.

"The more we learn, the more it appears the problem is not the program or the DOE guidance itself, but the way it is being applied," Mr. Rubio said, referring to the Education Department. "It may have created a culture discourages referral to law enforcement even in egregious cases like the #Parkland shooter."

Long before the attack in Parkland, Fla., the 2014 discipline guidelines, which encouraged schools to examine their discipline disparities and to take stock of discriminatory policies, were already on Ms. DeVos's radar — but not because they were seen as a possible culprit in the next school shooting. Conservatives were using the Trump administration's effort to rein in federal overreach to reverse policies designed to protect against what the Obama administration had seen as discriminatory practices.

The "Rethink Discipline," package that Mr. Trump's commission will examine includes guidance that the Obama administration issued on the legal limitations on the use of restraints and seclusion, corporal punishment and equity for special education students.

In recent months, educators and policy experts from across the country have traveled to Washington to voice support for and opposition to the disciplinary guidance, in private meetings with officials at the Education Department and in a series of public forums.

At a briefing hosted by the United States Commission on Civil Rights, dozens of policy experts, researchers, educators and parents sounded off on the Obama-era discipline policy in a meeting that became so racially charged that some black attendees walked out.

Since the discipline guidelines were issued, conservatives have blamed the document for creating unsafe educational environments by pressuring schools to keep suspension numbers down to meet racial quotas, even if it meant ignoring troubling and criminal behavior. Teachers who sought suspensions or expulsions of minority students were painted as racists, conservatives maintained.

"Evidence is mounting that efforts to fight the school-to-prison pipeline is creating a school climate catastrophe and has if anything put at-risk students at greater risk," said Max Eden, a senior fellow at the conservative Manhattan Institute, who argued that teacher bias was not the driving force behind school discipline.

But proponents argued that racial bias was well documented.

When the guidance was issued, federal data found that African-American students without disabilities were more than three times as likely as their white peers without disabilities to be expelled or suspended, and that more than 50 percent of students who were involved in school-related arrests or who were referred to law enforcement were Hispanic or African-American.

"Children's safety also includes protection from oppression and bigotry and injustice," Daniel J. Losen, director of the Center for Civil Rights Remedies at the University of California at Los

Angeles's Civil Rights Project, wrote in testimony to the Civil Rights Commission. "Fear-mongering and rhetoric that criminalizes youth of color, children from poor families and children with disabilities should not be tolerated."

The Education and Justice Departments wrote in a 2014 Dear Colleague letter that discipline disparities could be caused by a range of factors, but the statistics in the federal data "are not explained by more frequent or more serious misbehavior by students of color." The departments also noted that several civil rights investigations had verified that minority students were disciplined more harshly than their white peers for the same infractions.

"In short, racial discrimination in school discipline is a real problem," the guidance said.

In recent months, Ms. DeVos has said change will be coming. She has already moved to rescind a regulation that protects against racial disparities in special education placements. Her goal, she said last month, was to be "sensitive to all of the parties involved."

In a bruising interview on "60 Minutes" on Sunday, Ms. DeVos said that the disproportionate discipline issue "comes down to individual kids." She declined to say whether she believed that black students disciplined more harshly for the same infraction were the victims of institutional racism.

"We're studying it carefully and are committed to making sure students have opportunity to learn in safe and nurturing environments," she said.

Ms. DeVos's office for civil rights also announced that it would scale back the scope of investigations, reversing an approach taken under the Obama administration to conduct exhaustive reviews of school districts' practices and data when a discrimination complaint was filed.

But Ms. DeVos's own administration has continued to find racial disparities. In November, the Education Department found that the Loleta Union Elementary School District in California doled out harsher treatment to Native American students than their white peers. For example, a Native American student received a one-day out-of-school suspension for slapping another student on the way to the bus, in what was that student's first disciplinary referral of the year. A white student received lunch detention for slapping two students on the same day — the student's fifth and sixth referrals that year.

While Mr. Cruz was repeatedly kicked out of class and ultimately expelled, it is unclear whether he was ever referred to the police for his behavior in school. However, Mr. Cruz was known to law enforcement, which never found cause to arrest him, and a report of troublesome behavior to the F.B.I. went unheeded.

The Broward County superintendent, Robert Runcie, said that Mr. Rubio's effort to connect the district's discipline policies to the Stoneman Douglas shooting was misguided.

"We're not going to dismantle a program that's been successful in the district because of false information that someone has put out there," Mr. Runcie said on Twitter. "We will neither manage nor lead by rumors."

Should Teachers Carry Guns?
Are Metal Detectors Helpful?
What Experts Say

BY ANEMONA HARTOCOLLIS AND JACEY FORTIN | FEB. 22, 2018

PAUL HANKINS keeps a box of smooth, colorful river stones — he calls them "fidgets" — in his classroom for students to hold when they need to soothe their nerves.

The stones also have a different purpose, as do the billiard balls and the plank from the old gym floor. They can all be used as weapons in an emergency.

"Before we go to the corner where everybody gets invisible, grab one of those," he tells his students at Silver Creek High School in Sellersburg, Ind. "We could cause one hell of a ruckus if we need to."

Mr. Hankins does not begrudge teachers who argue that they should be allowed to carry guns to class, especially in the wake of attacks like last week's shooting that killed 17 at Marjory Stoneman Douglas High School in Parkland, Fla.

For him, stones are better.

They put the fight in "Run, hide, fight," the mantra that he and countless other teachers are learning as lockdown drills become routine.

Yet experts are as divided as Mr. Hankins and his colleagues on how to protect students from violence or whether, for that matter, there is anything that can be done to prevent a determined attacker.

The latest shooting has intensified the debate over what tactics to use to protect against imminent danger: whether teachers should carry guns, or hide with their students; whether schools should invest in fancy security devices like door jammers or put more resources into crisis teams that could identify and intervene with troubled students. What follows is some of the discussion.

WHAT ABOUT TEACHERS CARRYING GUNS?

Most law enforcement experts argue that teachers should not carry guns. Civilians may be able to hit a bull's-eye at the shooting range, but they lack the tactical knowledge of handling weapons that trained law enforcement personnel get.

Accidents happen. Guns can fall out of holsters, be taken from the classroom or accidentally discharge.

"You don't want to have a gun that's available to a student or another worker who may have mental health issues," said Maureen S. Rush, vice president for public safety and superintendent of the Police Department at the University of Pennsylvania.

But some disagree.

Dave Workman, the senior editor of The Gun Mag and communications director of the Citizens Committee for the Right to Keep and Bear Arms, said arming guards or teachers could act as a deterrent so that no one had to draw a weapon in the first place.

"I understand the debate out there: 'Should this be the job of a teacher?' " he said.

"Why not? The teacher is going to be there," Mr. Workman said. "They become the first responder sometimes. It does take a while for police to respond to an incident."

The Parkland school had an armed sheriff's deputy who never encountered the gunman.

ARE METAL DETECTORS HELPFUL?

Metal detectors are unlikely to stop a gunman, experts say. But they can be useful in certain contexts, if, for instance, the school is in a neighborhood with high crime or gang activity, where students may try to bring guns or knives into school to defend themselves.

WHAT IS THE PURPOSE OF A LOCKDOWN DRILL?

In a lockdown drill, everyone in the school practices responding seamlessly to the presence of an intruder. Teachers and students go to a secure location, like a classroom, closet or storage area that can be locked, and move out of sight, away from windows or doors.

Speed is important. The typical gunman is like water, the experts said, following the path of least resistance. Typically, a gunman will not try to kick in a closed door, but will look for one with a crack of light showing.

"Within 20 or 30 seconds, I, as a bad guy, should have very little easy access to anybody," said David R. Connors, head of Connors Security Consulting Services in Spencerport, N.Y., and a former police officer. The locks or barricades on the doors do not need to be very strong, just enough to last until help can arrive.

The point of a lockdown drill is to know what to do automatically, without having to think.

"When something's going down, you will not respond from your head, you will respond from your stomach," Ms. Rush said. "You need to get that in your stomach. You need to know what instinctively you will do. That's got to be part of your psyche. So it requires constant training."

Different schools or districts may have different protocols. The important thing is that everyone, from teachers to students to parents, know what they are. "It has to be something that goes like clockwork," said Dr. Irwin Redlener, a professor of pediatrics and public health and the director of the National Center for Disaster Preparedness at Columbia University.

IF SOMEONE KNOCKS ON A LOCKED DOOR, SHOULD THEY BE ALLOWED IN?

It may be heart-wrenching, but don't open the door, experts say. A teacher has to think of the lives of the many who have moved to a safe place over the one person outside in the hallway who may bring danger in.

"You don't open that door until you know the police are on the other side," Ms. Rush said, adding, "You're doing it for the masses of kids."

WHAT SHOULD STUDENTS BE TOLD?

It depends on their age. "We don't have to scare the heck out of these kids," Mr. Connors said. "In a kindergarten through third-grade building, you might tell the kids, come over here and sit down next to the wall. Be nice and quiet. I'm going to read you a book. That's all the kids have to know."

Mr. Connors does not believe in making drills too realistic. "You don't have to have someone come over and try to kick in the door. I don't think that's constructive. With staff, yes. But not with kids."

IS IT A GOOD IDEA TO LET STUDENTS USE CELLPHONES?

Phones should be put on silent, not even vibrating. "Texting is fine," Ms. Rush said. "You want to be invisible, and you want silence."

Ms. Rush said she was alarmed by the students who took videos while hiding from the gunman in Parkland, not because she disapproved of the video, but because it changed their mentality. "That could be taking them out of their survivor mode," she said.

WHAT ABOUT IDENTIFYING A TROUBLED STUDENT?

The experts vary on whether this is possible. Some say that students who become violent are often not the ones who seem most troubled or who make the most noise. "The perpetrators are very often not the bullies or the guys roughing people up," Mr. Connors said. "Quite often, it's the guy who is quiet. In hindsight, they'll go back and find that there's some family or mental health issue."

Others say that schools can do more to enlist students to help identify troubled classmates. Social media can be an early warning system, the experts say. Students may express their violent thoughts there, as did Nikolas Cruz, who has been charged in the Florida shooting, according to law enforcement officials.

"These kids are begging us to stop them," said Amy Klinger, a co-founder of the Educator's School Safety Network, who consults on school safety from the perspective of the former teacher and principal that she is. "We just have to be better at picking up the warning signs."

The schools alone cannot do it. Arguably, Dr. Klinger said, the failure to identify Mr. Cruz as troubled was a failure of the entire community, along with law enforcement agencies that had been warned about him.

"A school can identify the individual of concern, but they didn't create that individual," Dr. Klinger said. "So yeah, there is a role that the community and parents and our society has to play in identifying and dealing with those individuals as well."

WHAT ABOUT INVESTING IN SECURITY DEVICES?

Law enforcement experts suggest hardening the perimeter, that is, putting up security cameras, door buzzers, gates, and other barricades or high-tech devices.

But they say that buzzers are not enough, especially at arrival and dismissal times when hundreds of students may be milling around.

"After Sandy Hook, a lot of schools got very panicky and bought $5,000 buzzer systems," Dr. Klinger said. "They bought the system that was breached by the intruder in the first 30 seconds of Sandy Hook. He shot out the door and walked into the school. So your buzzer system did absolutely no good."

Ms. Rush said that everyone at the front office should be informed when a student has been suspended or expelled. A photo should be posted, and they should call 911 if the person appears.

"This happens in corporate America all the time," she said. "Workplace violence, where the person comes back and wants to kill the boss."

Dr. Klinger said that schools should invest in teachers who mingle with students in the lobby or in hallways as a way to learn about troubling behavior that may be brewing.

Even in a large school, the experts said, doors need to be manned by someone who knows the students and will recognize anyone who looks out of place. Dr. Klinger said that this should be a teacher, who relates to the students, not a security guard.

"If you want to take this to the extreme, you can ensure the safety of kids by locking them in a cell, but that's a prison," Dr. Klinger said. "This is not a prison. It's not a shopping mall."

WHAT IF YOU CAN'T RUN OR HIDE?

Cultivate the survivor mentality, experts said. Fight. "If he's coming no matter what, if you got that one guy who starts breaking the door out, you take every object in the room and you beat the hell out of him to disarm him, because you're going to die if you don't," Ms. Rush said. "So you might as well take your chances of trying to fight."

Ms. Rush gave the example of a professor who, as a gunman approached, took his phone out to look at pictures of his children one last time before he died. "But a female student jumped and ran and locked the door. She had survivor instinct."

Letting American Kids Die

OPINION | BY DAVID LEONHARDT | FEB. 17, 2018

IN A SANDY HOOK, CONN., firehouse in 2012, not long after another school shooting, a group of terrified parents was waiting for news about their children. Connecticut's governor, Dan Malloy, then walked into the room and quietly told them, "If you haven't been reunited with your loved one by now, that is not going to happen." The room convulsed in grief.

That scene remains haunting because it hints at both the agony and the scale of mass shootings. Children keep dying. And our country won't do anything about it.

The United States, to put it bluntly, has grown callous about the lives of its children. We mourn their deaths when they happen, of course. But it's an empty mourning, because it is not accompanied by any effort to prevent more suffering — including straightforward steps that every other affluent nation has taken.

Guns are a big part of the callousness, but only a part of it. They are one of three main reasons the United States has become "the most dangerous of wealthy nations for a child to be born into," according to a study in Health Affairs. The other two are vehicle crashes and infant mortality.

This country suffers almost 21,000 "excess deaths" each year. That's how many children and teenagers would be spared if the United States had an average mortality rate for a rich country.

Here's another way to think about those 21,000: Imagine the Sandy Hook firehouse, filled with the devastated families of 20 children. Now add two other Sandy Hook firehouses, each with 20 more families receiving the worst possible news. Now imagine that scene repeating itself every day, year after year after year.

Our outlier status is relatively new, too. In the 1960s, the United States had a child-mortality rate slightly below that of other rich countries. So it's not as if the problem stems from an immutable American characteristic.

Other countries are simply trying harder to keep their children alive. They have studied major causes of death and then attacked them, in an evidence-based way.

What would such an approach look like in this country?

On guns, it would start with universal background checks and tighter semiautomatic restrictions. The United States is always likely to have gun deaths, given the sheer number of guns, but we could have many fewer.

On vehicle deaths, we could mostly copy what other countries have already done: enforce speeding laws, crack down on "buzzed" driving, encourage seatbelts. Because we have lagged, American roads have gone from being average on safety to being the most dangerous in the affluent world.

On infant mortality, the solutions are more complex. They probably involve patching up the flawed safety net. Notably, infant mortality has fallen in states that expanded Medicaid under Obamacare — and risen slightly in states that didn't, according to a study in the American Journal of Public Health.

When you look at the big causes of preventable childhood death, it's hard not to notice a political pattern. One party — the Republican Party — is blocking sensible gun laws. The same party has been trying to take away people's health insurance. And while traffic safety is a bipartisan problem, blue states are generally trying harder than red states.

All of which is a good reminder to get politically engaged. If the current crop of politicians isn't willing to protect our children from harm, let's replace them with politicians — from either party — who are.

CHAPTER 5

The Future: Student Action Shaping the Debate

The National Rifle Association has always had energy and strategy. Its success over the decades in lobbying to loosen any gun restrictions is undeniable and largely the result of massive spending on campaign contributions to Republican lawmakers. But the Parkland shooting energized a national movement. First, the cycle of tragedy played itself out — disbelief, anguish and heartbreak. But then, a new outrage emerged, a collection of strong, young voices.

A 'Mass Shooting Generation' Cries Out for Change

BY AUDRA D. S. BURCH, PATRICIA MAZZEI AND JACK HEALY | FEB. 16, 2018

PARKLAND, FLA. — Delaney Tarr, a high school senior, cannot remember a time when she did not know about school shootings.

So when a fire alarm went off inside Marjory Stoneman Douglas High School and teachers began screaming "Code red!" as confused students ran in and out of classrooms, Ms. Tarr, 17, knew what to do. Run to the safest place in the classroom — in this case, a closet packed with 19 students and their teacher.

"I've been told these protocols for years," she said. "My sister is in middle school — she's 12 — and in elementary school, she had to do code red drills."

This is life for the children of the mass shooting generation. They were born into a world reshaped by the 1999 attack at Columbine High School in Colorado, and grew up practicing active shooter drills and huddling through lockdowns. They talked about threats and safety steps with their parents and teachers. With friends, they wondered darkly whether it could happen at their own school, and who might do it.

Now, this generation is almost grown up. And when a gunman killed 17 people this week at Stoneman Douglas High in Parkland, Fla., the first response of many of their classmates was not to grieve in silence, but to speak out. Their urgent voices — in television interviews, on social media, even from inside a locked school office as they hid from the gunman — are now rising in the national debate over gun violence in the aftermath of yet another school shooting.

While many politicians after the shooting were focused on mental health and safety, some vocal students at Stoneman Douglas High showed no reluctance in drawing attention to gun control.

SAUL MARTINEZ FOR THE NEW YORK TIMES

Students sought to reunite with their parents after the shooting at Marjory Stoneman Douglas High School on Wednesday.

They called out politicians over Twitter, with one student telling Senator Marco Rubio, a Florida Republican, "YOU DON'T UNDERSTAND." Shortly after the shooting, Cameron Kasky, a junior at the school, and a few friends started a "Never Again" campaign on Facebook that shared stories and perspectives from other students who survived the rampage.

On a day when the funerals of the shooting victims began here, more than a dozen schools from Massachusetts to Iowa to Michigan were shut down in response to copycat threats and social media interpreted in the worst light. A college near Seattle was on lockdown for several hours on Friday after an unfounded report of gunfire and in at least one case an entire district closed down. Several students have been arrested, accused of phoning in threats to their schools.

At other high schools across the country, students rallied in solidarity with Stoneman Douglas High and staged walkouts to protest what they called Washington's inaction in protecting students and teachers. A gun control advocacy group, Moms Demand Action, said it had been so overwhelmed with requests from students that it was setting up a parallel, student focused advocacy group.

"People say it's too early to talk about it," Mr. Kasky said. "If you ask me, it's way too late."

His argument reflects the words of other students who want action: The issue is not an abstraction to them. These are their murdered friends, their bloodstained schools, their upended lives.

Students said they did not want to cede the discussion over their lives to politicians and adult activists.

"We need to take it into our hands," Mr. Kasky said.

David Hogg, a 17-year-old student journalist who interviewed his classmates during the rampage in Parkland, said he had thought about the possibility of a school shooting long before shots from an AR-15 started to blast through the hallways. As he huddled with fellow students, he stayed calm and decided to try to create a record of their thoughts and views that would live on, even if the worst happened to them.

"I recorded those videos because I didn't know if I was going to survive," he said in an interview here. "But I knew that if those videos survived, they would echo on and tell the story. And that story would be one that would change things, I hoped. And that would be my legacy."

It is a stark change from the moments that followed the Columbine shooting in April 1999, said Austin Eubanks, who survived the shooting. Mr. Eubanks and a friend hid under a table when the two teenage gunmen walked into the library and started shooting. Mr. Eubanks was wounded. His friend, Corey DePooter, was killed.

"There was nobody who took an activism stance," Mr. Eubanks said of Columbine's immediate aftermath. He said he began abusing opiates shortly after as a coping mechanism. "I just wanted to be left alone. I was so destabilized and traumatized."

Mr. Eubanks now helps run an addiction treatment center in Colorado and has sons of his own, aged 8 and 12. The oldest has asked why Columbine happened and whether he needs to be afraid, and Mr. Eubanks said he has tried to make the boys feel safe while also discussing how children can drift toward violence.

No matter how rare school shootings are for the vast majority of students, they have grown up in a world so attuned to these threats that high schoolers are now more conversant in the language of lockdowns and code red drills than their parents.

Spencer Collier, the police chief in Selma, Ala., was chatting recently with a group of high school students when they brought up mass shootings and pressed him about current trends and what law enforcement agencies were doing to address them. In Connecticut, Nathaniel Laske, a high school junior, said he had asked school administrators about the apparent absence of lockdown drills or a mass shooting plan in the event something happened during school theater productions.

"A lot of people aren't willing to talk about it," Mr. Laske said. "When you're part of a school community it makes you much more inclined to want to prevent things."

Nathanael Clark, a Stoneman Douglas High student, and his father, John, talked to the news media after Wednesday's shooting.

Soon after Amy Campbell-Oates, 16, heard about the Parkland shooting, she knew she wanted to try, in some small way, to influence the national discussion on gun violence. She and two friends organized a protest, made posters, and on Friday, they rallied with dozens of fellow students from South Broward High School.

They carried signs that read "It Could've Been Us," and "Your Silence is Killing Us," and "We Stand with Stoneman Douglas." They chanted, their collective voices rising as cars honked in support.

"We agreed that our politicians have to do more than say thoughts and prayers," Ms. Campbell-Oates said. "We want voters to know that midterms are coming up. Some of us can't vote yet but we want to get to the people that can to vote in common sense laws, ban assault rifles and require mental health checks before gun purchases."

Tyra Hemans, a senior at Stoneman Douglas High, made a poster, too, emblazoned with the word "ENOUGH." On Friday, Ms. Hemans attended the funeral for Meadow Pollack, one of the 17 people killed, and then she spoke about her desire to see President Trump when he visits the area.

"I want our politicians to stop thinking about money and start thinking about all these lives we have lost," she said. "I want to talk with him about changing these laws. Seventeen people are dead, killed in minutes."

National School Walkout: Thousands Protest Against Gun Violence Across the U.S.

BY VIVIAN YEE AND ALAN BLINDER | MARCH 14, 2018

A MONTH AGO, hundreds of teenagers ran for their lives from the hallways and classrooms of Marjory Stoneman Douglas High School, where 17 students and staff had been shot to death.

On Wednesday, driven by the conviction that they should never have to run from guns again, they walked.

So did their peers. In New York City, in Chicago, in Atlanta and Santa Monica; at Columbine High School and in Newtown, Conn.; and in many more cities and towns, students left school by the hundreds and the thousands at 10 a.m., sometimes in defiance of school authorities, who seemed divided and even flummoxed about how to handle their emptying classrooms.

The first major coordinated action of the student-led movement for gun control marshaled the same elements that had defined it ever since the Parkland shooting: eloquent young voices, equipped with symbolism and social media savvy, riding a resolve as yet untouched by cynicism.

"We have grown up watching more tragedies occur and continuously asking: Why?" said Kaylee Tyner, a 16-year-old junior at Columbine High School outside Denver, where 13 people were killed in 1999, inaugurating, in the public consciousness, the era of school shootings. "Why does this keep happening?"

Even after a year of near continuous protesting — for women, for the environment, for immigrants and more — the emergence of people not even old enough to drive as a political force has been particularly arresting, unsettling a gun control debate that had seemed impervious to other factors.

In Florida, where students from Stoneman Douglas High and other schools had rallied in the state capital, the governor signed a bill last

Students rallied for gun control legislation in Manhattan on Wednesday.

week that raised the minimum age to purchase a firearm to 21 and extended the waiting period to three days.

On a national level, the students have not had the same impact. This week, President Trump abandoned gun control proposals that the Republican-led Congress had never even inched toward supporting.

But, for one day at least, the students commanded the country's airwaves, Twitter feeds and Snapchat stories.

Principals and superintendents seemed disinclined to stop them. Some were outright supportive, though others warned that students would face disciplinary consequences for leaving school. At many schools, teachers and parents joined in.

Wreathed in symbolism, the walkouts generally lasted for 17 minutes, one for each of the Parkland victims. Two more nationwide protests are set to take place on March 24 and on April 20, the anniversary of the Columbine shooting.

On a soccer field burned yellow by the Colorado sun, Ms. Tyner stood alongside hundreds of her fellow students, who waved signs — "This is our future," one said — and released red, white and blue balloons.

Yet in many places, for many students, Wednesday was just Wednesday, and class went on. Even at Columbine, the embrace of the gun control movement was not universal.

"People say it's all about gun control, it's all about, 'We should ban guns,'" said Caleb Conrad, 16, a junior, who stayed in class. "But that's not the real issue here. The real issue is the people who are doing it."

In the one-school rural community of Potosi, Wis., no student group had organized a protest. After a handful of students expressed some interest, the school decided to hold an assembly at 10 a.m. to talk about school safety measures and the value of being kind to one another.

At 10 a.m., one student, a female freshman, left the building alone.

Throughout the assembly, she sat by herself outside, by a flagpole, for 17 minutes. She appeared to be praying, said the principal, Mike Uppena, adding that she was not in trouble for leaving.

Officials in Lafayette Parish, La., initially said that students could participate in the day's events, believing that it was appropriate to honor the Florida victims. But when it became clear there was a political motive to the walkout, a torrent of complaints from the local community led the school board to adopt a new plan: a minute of silence.

Dozens of students walked out anyway.

OUT OF CLASS AND INTO THE STREETS

In some places, demonstrators chanted and held signs. At other schools, students stood in silence. In Atlanta, some students took a knee.

Thousands of New York City students converged on central locations — Columbus Circle, Battery Park, Brooklyn Borough Hall, Lincoln Center.

Gov. Andrew M. Cuomo, a Democrat, stretched out on the sidewalk as part of a "die-in" with students in Zuccotti Park in Lower Manhattan, the former home of the Occupy Wall Street protests.

Hundreds sat in the middle of West 62nd Street for several minutes before rising to their feet and shouting, "No more violence." A cry of "Trump Tower!" sent dozens of protesters marching toward the Trump International Hotel and Tower across Broadway. Onlookers gave them fist-bumps.

In Washington, thousands left their classrooms in the city and its suburbs and marched to the Capitol steps, their high-pitched voices battling against the stiff wind: "Hey-hey, ho-ho, the N.R.A. has got to go!" One sign said: "Fix This, Before I Text My Mom from Under A Desk."

Members of Congress, overwhelmingly Democratic, emerged from the Capitol to meet them. Trailed by aides and cameras, some legislators high-fived the children in the front rows, others took selfies, and nearly all soon learned that the young protesters had no idea who they were.

Except, of course, for "BERNIE SANDERS!" which the protesters screamed at the Vermont senator, as well at some other white-haired, bespectacled legislators.

Asked by reporters about the walkouts, Raj Shah, Mr. Trump's deputy press secretary, said the president "shares the students' concerns about school safety" and cited his support for mental health and background check improvements.

As the hours passed, the walkouts moved west across the country.

"It's 10 o'clock," said a man on the intercom at Perspectives Charter Schools on Chicago's South Side. With that, hundreds of students streamed out of their classrooms and into the neighborhood, marching past modest brick homes, a Walgreens and multiple churches.

Several current and former Perspectives students have been killed in recent years, the school president said.

"You see different types of violence going on," said Armaria Broyles, a junior who helped lead the walkout and whose older brother was killed in a shooting. "We all want a good community and we all want to make a change."

At Santa Monica High School in Southern California, teachers guided hundreds of students to the football field. It felt like a cross between a political rally and pep rally, with dozens of students wearing orange T-shirts, the color of the gun control movement, and #neveragain scrawled onto their arms in black eyeliner.

"It is our duty to win," Roger Gawne, a freshman and one of the protest organizers, yelled to the crowd.

STAYING SILENT, FOR THE OPPOSITE REASON

Although the walkouts commanded attention on cable television and social media for much of Wednesday, it also was clear that many students did not participate, especially in rural and conservative areas where gun control is not popular.

At Bartlesville High School in Bartlesville, Okla., where hundreds of students walked out of class last month to protest cuts in state education funding, nothing at all happened at 10 a.m. lor, said of the gun protest.

In Iowa, Russell Reiter, superintendent of the Oskaloosa Community School District, suggested that temperatures below 40 degrees may have encouraged students to stay indoors, but he also said that "students here are just not interested in what is going on in bigger cities."

There was opposition even in liberal Santa Monica. Just after the organizers of the walkout there read the names of the Parkland victims, another student went on stage, grabbed the microphone and shouted "Support the Second Amendment!" before he was called off by administrators.

'WE NEED MORE THAN JUST 17 MINUTES'

Some of the day's most poignant demonstrations happened at schools whose names are now synonymous with shootings.

Watched by a phalanx of reporters, camera operators and supporters, hundreds of students crowded onto the football field at Stoneman Douglas High shortly after 10 a.m.

A month after the Feb. 14 shooting, notes of condolence, fading flowers and stuffed toys, damp from recent rain, still lay on the grass outside the school and affixed to metal fences.

The walkout was allowed by the school, but several students said they were warned that they would not be permitted back onto the campus for the day if they left school grounds. Despite the warning, a couple of hundred students marched to a nearby park for another demonstration.

"We need more than just 17 minutes," Nicolle Montgomerie, 17, a junior, said as she walked toward the park.

An email from the school soon went out telling students they could return.

In Newtown, Conn., where 26 people were killed at Sandy Hook Elementary School in 2012, hundreds of students at Newtown High School gathered in a parking lot near the football field. Two hours later, it was Columbine's turn.

A WORD OR TWO FROM GUN RIGHTS GROUPS

Shortly after the walkouts began, the National Rifle Association said on Twitter, "Let's work together to secure our schools and stop school violence."

But the next tweet left no doubt as to where the N.R.A. stood on the message of the protests. It said, "I'll control my own guns, thank you. #2A #NRA" atop a photo of an AR-15, the kind of high-powered rifle used at Stoneman Douglas High and in other mass shootings.

The Gun Owners of America, a smaller organization often seen as more militant than the N.R.A., was more defiant.

The group urged its supporters to call their elected officials to oppose gun control measures like Fix NICS, which is intended to improve reporting by state and federal agencies to the criminal background check system. "We could win or lose the gun control battle in the next 96 hours," the group said on Twitter.

The group also celebrated "the pro-gun students who are not supporting their anti-gun counterparts."

WARNINGS FROM SCHOOLS, NOT ALWAYS HEEDED

Some schools accommodated or even encouraged the protests. But others warned that they would mark students who left as absent, or even suspend them.

In Cobb County, Ga., near Atlanta, the threat of punishment did not keep scores of Walton High School students from standing in silence on the football field for 170 seconds. A school district spokesman did not respond to a request for comment on what would happen to the students.

Noelle Ellerson Ng, associate executive director for policy and advocacy for AASA, the association of the nation's superintendents, said that schools had to balance the First Amendment rights of students with their other responsibilities, including safety.

Indeed, several protests were canceled because of threats of the same kind of violence the students were demonstrating against. A demonstration at Broughton High School in Raleigh, N.C., was called off when the principal learned of what she later described as "a false rumor of a threat and a post on social media that caused unnecessary fear among our school community."

REPORTING WAS CONTRIBUTED BY JESS BIDGOOD, JULIE BOSMAN, SYDNEY EMBER, DANA GOLDSTEIN, ANEMONA HARTOCOLLIS, SEAN KEENAN, NICK MADIGAN, JENNIFER MEDINA, JOHN PERAGINE, RICK ROJAS, STEPHANIE SAUL, NATE SCHWEBER, MITCH SMITH, KATE TAYLOR, JULIE TURKEWITZ AND ELIZABETH WILLIAMSON.

Florida Shooting Survivor Wants Action: 'We're Children. You Guys Are the Adults.'

BY JULIE TURKEWITZ AND NIRAJ CHOKSHI | FEB. 15, 2018

PARKLAND, FLA. — David Hogg stood in the Florida sun on Thursday, not far from his now shuttered school, and described the events of the day before.

Mr. Hogg, 17, a lanky senior at Marjory Stoneman Douglas High School and the student news director there, was in his environmental science class when a single shot rang out, echoing down the hallways.

His teacher pulled the door shut, but soon the fire alarm began to blare. Then, he said, came the sound of thousands of student footsteps, and Mr. Hogg and his classmates raced out the door, joining a giant wave of teenagers.

"There was a tsunami of people running in one specific direction away from something," he said, "and that's what we were doing. It was almost like there was a shark coming along and we were a school of fish. And we were running from that armed man."

A janitor appeared and began to wave. "Stop, stop!" he said. "Go over here!"

Then the school chef opened a door to her office, Mr. Hogg said, and hurried the teenagers in — first 10, then 20, then some 30 or 40 students crowded in the office. They shut off the lights. And then students turned to their phones, and began the horrifying experience of watching a school shooting unfold at their own school — through the news apps on their phones.

While they were hiding, Mr. Hogg proceeded to interview his classmates on camera about their beliefs on gun policy.

Mr. Hogg's younger sister, 14, was also in the building. Two of her best friends were among the 17 people who died, he said.

"On a national scale, I'm not surprised at all," he said of the shooting. "And that's just sad. The fact that a student is not surprised that there was another mass shooting — but this time it was at his school — says so much about the current state that our country is in, and how much has to be done."

The violence must stop, he said, issuing a call to pressure lawmakers to act to make schools safer.

"We need to do something. We need to get out there and be politically active. Congress needs to get over their political bias with each other and work toward saving children's lives."

In an interview with CNN earlier on Thursday, Mr. Hogg expressed his frustration with politicians in simpler terms: "We're children," he said. "You guys are the adults."

Kelsey Friend, a freshman at the school, appeared alongside Mr. Hogg on CNN, and grew emotional as she thanked a geography teacher who she said had saved her life.

"I will never forget the actions that he took for me and for fellow students of the classroom," she said through tears. "And if his family is watching this, please know that your son or your brother was an amazing person and I'm alive today because of him. Thank you."

Other students shared stories of the ordeal as well.

Sarah Crescitelli, a freshman, said Wednesday that she was in drama class when gunshots rang out. While hiding with about 40 others in a storage room, she texted her mother, telling her, "If I don't make it, I love you."

Others, who spoke to CNN, described how a large group hid in an R.O.T.C. room where they used Kevlar blankets from a marksmanship class for protection.

At a news conference on Thursday, Robert Runcie, the superintendent of Broward County Public Schools, called for a national conversation on passing "sensible" gun control laws.

"Our students are asking for that conversation," he said. "And I hope we can get it done in this generation. But if we don't, they will."

Don't Let My Classmates' Deaths Be in Vain

OPINION | BY CHRISTINE YARED | FEB. 18, 2018

PARKLAND, FLA. — I am a freshman at Marjory Stoneman Douglas High School in Parkland, Fla. In the days since the attack that killed 17 people here, I have continued replaying those terrifying moments in my head.

It began when a fire alarm went off just before school was supposed to end. We thought nothing of it. People in my finance class had already left, and I grabbed my backpack to evacuate. The next thing I knew I heard people running and shouting, and my teacher yelling at us to get back in the class.

I sprinted to her closet and crammed myself against shelves filled with papers and binders. The rest of the closet filled up with the other students. We thought it was an active shooter drill. It wasn't.

SAUL MARTINEZ FOR THE NEW YORK TIMES

Christine Yared in Parkland, Fla.

My phone flooded with messages from friends and family, from other states and other countries, asking if I was O.K. The world knew what was happening even before we did. I texted my sister to make sure everything was all right with her. I checked in with my friends, and most of them were safe, or had evacuated. I texted my family and told them that I loved them.

My classmates scoured the internet, searching for news about what was happening. We found out the shooter was in the freshman building, 50 feet away from our classroom. I was busy shaking in the corner of my little bunker, trying to calm my panic, while rumors about the shooter and the victims arrived by text and Snapchat. We could hear loud noises outside. Were they gunshots? We weren't sure.

After over an hour of confusion and heat, the police SWAT team finally came to get us.

We ran out with our phones in our pockets, and our hands over our heads. I have never run so fast. I met up with my friends and sat with them, still in shock. I saw kids crying, traumatized. At home it still didn't feel real. We tried to watch some TV to distract ourselves. We saw celebrities and politicians talking about our school. But it didn't feel like our school, it seemed like a movie, a dream, a nightmare.

My parents worked hard to leave war-torn Lebanon so that their children would never have to experience the violence and loss that they did. My dad was a first-aid volunteer with the Lebanese Red Cross. He continued his engineering education, worked for General Electric in France and was transferred to the United States. My family lived in Utah; Colorado, where I was born; Minnesota; and finally Florida. My parents chose Parkland to settle in because of Marjory Stoneman Douglas's stellar reputation, and because we thought that it was a safe place to live. But that isn't true anymore. The promise of safety and security failed us.

One week ago, nobody knew about the small suburb that was Parkland. Now every time I look up "Marjory Stoneman Douglas" on the internet, the top suggestion is "shooting."

My friends, classmates and teachers are dead. I see the media portraying them as good children who were smart and kind, but they were much more than that.

My friend Gina is dead. I had just talked to her that morning in art class. We laughed together, we sang together, we smiled together. We will never do that again. How could someone be this despicable? When I think about it, I start bawling.

We can't let innocent people's deaths be in vain. We need to work together beyond political parties to make sure this never happens again. We need tougher gun laws.

If a person is not old enough to be able to rent a car or buy a beer, then he should not be able to legally purchase a weapon of mass destruction. This could have been prevented. If the killer had been properly treated for his mental illness, maybe this would not have happened. If there were proper background checks, then those who should not have guns would not have them.

We need to vote for those who are for stricter laws and kick out those who won't take action. We need to expose the truth about gun violence and the corruption around guns. Please.

It's devastating that this happened on Valentine's Day, a day that's supposed to be about love. Take this as a sign to hug your loved ones and be sure to tell them you love them every day because you never know when it will be their last.

If you have any heart, or care about anyone or anything, you need to be an advocate for change. Don't let any more children suffer like we have. Don't continue this cycle. This may not seem relevant to you. But next time it could be your family, your friends, your neighbors. Next time, it could be you.

CHRISTINE YARED IS 15.

Will America Choose Its Children Over Guns?

OPINION | BY THE NEW YORK TIMES | FEB. 20, 2018

AS SURELY as there are camels' backs and straws to break them, moments arrive when citizens say they've had enough, when they rise up against political leaders who do not speak for them and whose moral fecklessness imperils lives. We may be witness to such a moment now with the protests by American teenagers sickened — and terrified — by the latest mass murder at the hands of someone with easy access to a weapon fit for a battlefield, not a school.

These kids have had enough. They've had enough of empty expressions of sympathy in the wake of the sort of atrocities they've grown up with, like last week's mass shooting that took 17 lives at a high school in Parkland, Fla. Enough of the ritualistic mouthing of thoughts and prayers for the victims. Enough of living in fear that they could be next in the cross hairs of a well-armed deranged killer, even with all the active shooter drills and lockdowns they've gone through. Enough of craven politicians who kneel before the National Rifle Association and its cynically fundamentalist approach to the Second Amendment.

They are asking in what kind of country are children sent off to school with bulletproof book bags strapped to their backs — capable, one manufacturer, Bullet Blocker, says, of "stopping a .357 Magnum, .44 Magnum, 9mm, .45 caliber hollow point ammunition and more."

"I was born 13 months after Columbine," a 12th grader named Faith Ward said on Monday, referring to the school massacre in Littleton, Colo., in 1999, the dawn of the modern wave of school shootings. Ms. Ward spoke to a television reporter at an anti-gun demonstration outside her school in Plantation, Fla. "This is all I have ever known," she said, "this culture of being gunned down for no reason, and this culture of people saying, 'Oh, let's send thoughts and prayers' for three days, and then moving on. And I'm tired of it."

So are we all.

It is too soon to tell if this righteous anger augurs a sustained youth movement for gun sanity, going beyond the occasional protest. We hope it does. It's time, once again, for America to listen to its children. Who among us have more at stake than they?

Sensible young people have it in their power to make their senseless elders take heed — and act. We saw it happen during the Vietnam War half a century ago. Young people, initially reviled by establishment forces as unwashed, longhaired traitors, energized an antiwar movement that swept the country and, even if it took years, ultimately ended America's misguided adventure in Southeast Asia.

To be effective, any movement needs a realistic program, not mere emotion. Otherwise, it risks coming and going in a flash with little to show for itself. A tighter federal system of background checks is a start, to better monitor would-be gun buyers with mental illness, for example, or histories of gun violence. Such a program should also include reinstating a nationwide ban on assault weapons — a state measure died in the Florida Legislature Tuesday — and ending an absurd prohibition against using federal public health funds to study gun violence.

Even President Trump, who told an N.R.A. convention last April that "you have a true friend and champion in the White House," has signaled he might be willing to improve the system. The Washington Post reported that after Mr. Trump saw the coverage of the student protesters, he asked Mar-a-Lago guests whether he should do more about gun control. On Tuesday, he ordered that regulations be written to ban bump stocks, devices that can make an automatic weapon out of a semiautomatic. Beyond that, though, it's hard to tell if he means business when he says he's open to more thorough background checks. Steadfastness is not a Trump hallmark.

However, if young people channeling this angry moment remain steadfast, they might not only force his hand but also stiffen the resolve of other elected officials and candidates. Horrific school shootings aside, they are vulnerable every day to gun mayhem at a stomach-churning rate. The journal Pediatrics reported last June that gunfire, each week, kills an average of 25 children ages 17 and under. A 2016 study in The American Journal of Medicine calculated that among two dozen of the world's wealthiest nations, this country alone accounted for 91 percent of firearms deaths among children 14 and under.

What the young protesters are saying now is: Put down the guns. We're your children.

How can anyone not heed their pained voices?

As Victims Are Mourned in Florida, a Search for Solace, and Action

BY AUDRA D. S. BURCH, NICK MADIGAN, RICHARD FAUSSET AND
JULIE TURKEWITZ | FEB. 18, 2018

CORAL SPRINGS, FLA. — Scott J. Beigel, a geography teacher at Marjory Stoneman Douglas High School, shepherded his students into the safety of a classroom Wednesday afternoon as a gunman roamed the halls, shooting, killing.

Mr. Beigel, 35, was fatally shot before he could lock the classroom door.

Four days later, hundreds of people filled a contemporary synagogue in Boca Raton to capacity, remembering Mr. Beigel not only for his final act of selflessness, but for an entire life in service of others.

"Scott's life was not that moment; Scott's heroism was not that incident," said his father, Michael Schulman. "Scott's heroism was his entire life."

On the first Sunday after a local high school lost 17 of its own, mourners said farewell at funerals, a call for action grew louder and a pastor implored his congregation not to lose faith.

"Our world is broken, but Jesus is not," Pastor Eddie Bevill of the Parkridge Church told the congregation, in reaction to the statements some students have made about the futility of prayer as a response to gun violence. "We pray that in the midst of the pain we are experiencing, that we can know you, Jesus."

Pastor Bevill also asked his flock to pray for the suspect in the shooting, Nikolas Cruz, although he did not mention Mr. Cruz's name or ask that he be forgiven.

At the high school, about a mile away from the church, a group of grief-stricken teenage survivors vowed to change the laws that allowed Mr. Cruz to get hold of an assault weapon that the authorities say he used to slaughter his former classmates.

In a movement that has been building since the massacre last week, student organizers said on Sunday that they would mount a demonstration next month in Washington called March For Our Lives. Their mission is to pivot America's long-running gun control debate — which tends to flare up with each mass shooting and then dissipate — toward meaningful action.

"We want this to stop. We need this to stop. We are protecting guns more than people," said Emma González, 18, one of five core organizers, whose impassioned speech at a rally in Fort Lauderdale on Saturday drew national attention. "We are not trying to take people's guns away; we are trying to make sure we have gun safety."

Ms. González, a senior at the school, said the group was inviting elected officials "from any side of the political spectrum" to join the movement. But she said: "We don't want anybody who is funded by the N.R.A. We want people who are going to be on the right side of history."

The organizers hope the march, scheduled for March 24, will attract students from across the country, and they say more protests are planned.

"Our hearts are heavy, we are overburdened, and we are incapable of holding the weight of grief that is upon us, but that is even more true of the families of the deceased," Pastor Bevill said. He then read aloud the names of the dead, as congregants wiped tears and held their arms aloft.

In the afternoon, hundreds of family and friends packed a hotel ballroom to honor the memory of Jaime Guttenberg, 14. Mourners heard from cousins, a favorite teacher and her parents, each offering glowing stories that were painful to hear. Jaime loved to dance. She loved the color orange. She loved her two dogs, Charlie and Cooper. Her favorite song was "Rewrite the Stars," and on the weekends, she volunteered to help people with special needs.

Fred Guttenberg talked about watching the television show "iCarly" together. He said she was a fighter whose energy could fill a room.

Mr. Guttenberg's eulogy ended in anger and a standing ovation. He vowed to fight gun violence, and admonished President Trump for a Saturday night Twitter post that accused the F.B.I. of missing "signals" of Wednesday's deadly rampage because of what the president characterized as the agency's preoccupation with the Russian investigation.

Mr. Beigel, one of three faculty members killed in the attack, had only worked for the school for a few months, but Denise Reed, an assistant principal, said she knew Mr. Beigel was a perfect match for the school "in definitely less than two or three minutes" after he began his interview for the job in the spring of 2017.

Mr. Schulman said that Mr. Beigel would not have believed that so many people would turn out to celebrate his life. "Eh, they just came for the food," Mr. Schulman imagined Mr. Beigel saying.

The funeral for another student, Meadow Pollack, 18, was held on Friday. Her relatives, classmates, Governor Rick Scott of Florida and many others were crowded in every corner of the Congregation Kol Tikvah synagogue, about a mile from the school.

Tears slipped from behind dark sunglasses as Rabbi Bradd Boxman recalled a girl who shone "like a star."

"I'm not here to explain any of this," he said. "I can't tell you why Meadow died the way that she did."

Ms. Pollack's boyfriend, Brandon Schoengrund, spoke about his "princess," his shoulders slumped in pain. And her father, Andrew Pollack, stood before the crowd and addressed the gunman.

"You. Killed. My. Kid." he said, one word at a time, his voice booming through the synagogue in grief and rage. "My kid is dead. It goes through my head all day. And night. I keep hearing it over and over."

"How does this happen to my beautiful, smart, loving daughter?" he said. "She is everything. If we could learn one thing from this tragedy, it's that our everythings are not safe when we send them to school."

The room heaved with sobbing teenagers as Ms. Pollack's coffin was wheeled out for burial.

Parents and Students Plead With Trump: 'How Many Children Have to Get Shot?'

BY JULIE HIRSCHFELD DAVIS | FEB. 21, 2018

WASHINGTON — An anguished father mourning his 18-year-old daughter vented his anger and pleaded for safer schools.

A fear-stricken student who watched classmates die last week wept openly as he called for banning assault weapons.

A mother who lost her 6-year-old son in a school shooting just over five years ago warned that more parents would lose their children if President Trump did not act, adding, "Don't let that happen on your watch."

One by one at the White House on Wednesday afternoon, survivors of school shootings and family members of victims shared their stories and their calls to action. The extraordinary public exchange with the president gave voice to an intensely emotional debate over how to respond to the latest gun massacre in an American school.

A week after a gunman opened fire with an AR-15-style assault rifle at Marjory Stoneman Douglas High School in Parkland, Fla., killing 17 people and prompting a rash of student-driven lobbying for new gun restrictions, Mr. Trump met for more than an hour with grieving people in search of solutions. News cameras captured the unusual listening session, revealing an emotional give-and-take between a president and private citizens that is typically shielded from public view.

Mr. Trump used the event to pitch his own ideas about how to prevent such debacles in the future, polling the group about whether they supported allowing teachers and other school employees to carry concealed weapons, an idea he said could have halted the carnage in Parkland.

"That coach was very brave, saved a lot of lives, I suspect," Mr. Trump said, apparently referring to Aaron Feis, a coach at Stoneman

Douglas who reportedly died using his body as a shield to protect students. "But if he had a firearm, he wouldn't have had to run, he would have shot and that would have been the end of it."

Mr. Trump said he would press to strengthen background checks for people buying guns and press for enhanced mental health measures. "We're going to go very strongly into age — age of purchase," he added, appearing to refer to a proposal to set an age threshold for buying certain weapons, including the AR-15.

But in a session that began as a subdued conversation and sometimes descended into tears and shouting, policy proposals were overshadowed by raw expressions of fear, anger and sorrow.

"We're here because my daughter has no voice — she was murdered last week, and she was taken from us, shot nine times," said Andrew Pollack, whose daughter Meadow was one of the 17 killed in Parkland. "How many schools, how many children have to get shot? It stops here, with this administration and me, because I'm not going to sleep until it's fixed."

Most of the students and parents invited from the Florida school appeared to support Mr. Trump, many of them prefacing their comments with praise for his leadership. But even fans of the president vented anger and desperation, laying the challenge of responding to the tragedy at his feet.

"It should have been one school shooting, and we should have fixed it — and I'm pissed," said Mr. Pollack, the only parent of a child killed in Parkland who was at the session, raising his voice as he looked at Mr. Trump. "Because my daughter, I'm not going to see again."

Samuel Zeif, 18, told of texting his parents and brothers from the second floor of Stoneman Douglas, believing that he would be killed, and he dissolved into tears as he begged the president, "Let's never let this happen again — please, please."

"I don't understand why I can still go in a store and buy a weapon of war, an A-R," Mr. Zeif said, referring to the AR-15 rifle. "How is it that easy to buy this type of weapon? How do we not stop this after

Columbine, after Sandy Hook? I'm sitting with a mother who lost her son. It's still happening."

Mr. Trump, who has often struggled to express empathy in the face of tragedy, appeared moved by the personal stories, even as he asked repeatedly whether anyone in the ornate room at the White House knew how such horrors could be prevented.

"I know you've been through a lot — most of you have been through a lot more than you ever thought possible," Mr. Trump said, seated in a circle with students and parents. "All I can say is that we're fighting hard for you, and we will not stop."

"I grieve for you," Mr. Trump added. "To me, there could be nothing worse than what you've gone through."

During the session, Mr. Trump held a card that appeared to remind him of the basics of compassion when dealing with grieving survivors. "What would you most want me to know about your experience?" read one handwritten note on the card, captured in photographs of the event. "I hear you," read another.

Mr. Pollack said he did not favor adopting new gun restrictions, but pleaded for Democrats and Republicans to come together to create new school safety measures.

"It's not about gun laws right now — that's another fight, another battle," he said. "We need our children safe."

Yet the subtext of the discussion was a contentious debate over gun restrictions and an all-too-familiar cycle of outrage, activism and promises of action, and then the inevitable inertia of Washington because of the opposition by the National Rifle Association and its allies.

Mr. Trump, a strident defender of gun rights who ran for office with the strong backing of the N.R.A., has come under immense pressure to endorse new gun limits after the Parkland massacre. The mass shooting has prompted a wave of youth activism that has reverberated from South Florida to Washington, where hundreds of students gathered outside the White House gates on Wednesday before the listening session, chanting, "Enough is enough!" and, "Hands up! — Don't shoot!"

Mark Barden, who lost his 7-year-old son Daniel at Sandy Hook Elementary School in Newtown, Conn., in 2012, said it was futile to believe Congress would act on new policies.

"We tried this legislative approach," said Mr. Barden, a founder and managing director of Sandy Hook Promise, a nonprofit advocacy group created after the massacre. "I've been in this building before many times, wringing our hands, pleading with legislators — 'What can we do?' — until we finally said we have to go home and do this ourselves."

He and Nicole Hockley, who lost her 6-year-old son Dylan at Sandy Hook, pressed Mr. Trump to consider prevention programs that train schools and educators to identify students in crisis and intervene before they attempt to harm themselves or others.

"Rather than arm them with a firearm," Ms. Hockley said of teachers, "I would rather arm them with the knowledge of how to prevent these acts from happening in the first place."

TOM BRENNER/THE NEW YORK TIMES

President Trump held a card of notes during the listening session on Wednesday.

One of Mr. Pollack's sons, Hunter, said he would prefer that educators carried weapons, arguing that more firearms on campus would lead to safer schools.

Yet it was the emotional appeals that appeared to have more influence on Mr. Trump.

Mr. Barden pulled out a photograph of his son showing a gap-toothed grin.

Mr. Pollack spoke movingly of "my beautiful daughter I'm never going to see again."

Ms. Hockley implored the president not to allow another massacre of children on his watch, saying: "Consider your own children. You don't want to be me — no parent does."

As he ended the session, Mr. Trump promised their stories would not go unheard or unaddressed.

"Thank you for pouring out your hearts," he said. "Because the world is watching, and we're going to come up with a solution."

In Wake of Florida Massacre, Gun Control Advocates Look to Connecticut

BY LISA W. FODERARO AND KRISTIN HUSSEY | FEB. 17, 2018

IN THE AFTERMATH of the rampage at Sandy Hook Elementary School in Newtown, where 20 children and six educators were killed in 2012, state lawmakers in Connecticut set out to draft some of the toughest gun measures in the country.

They largely succeeded — significantly expanding an existing ban on the sale of assault weapons, prohibiting the sale of magazines with more than 10 rounds and requiring the registration of existing assault rifles and higher-capacity magazines. The state also required background checks for all firearms sales and created a registry of weapons offenders, including those accused of illegally possessing a firearm.

Now, in the wake of another wrenching shooting rampage — this one at a high school in Parkland, Fla., that killed 17 — and in the absence of any federal action, gun-control advocates, Democratic politicians and others are pointing to the success of states like Connecticut in addressing the spiraling toll of gun violence.

Analyses by the Giffords Law Center to Prevent Gun Violence show that, with few exceptions, states with the strictest gun-control measures, including California, Connecticut, New Jersey and New York, have the lowest rates of gun deaths, while those with the most lax laws like Alabama, Alaska and Louisiana, have the highest. The center is named for former Representative Gabrielle Giffords, a Democratic lawmaker from Arizona who suffered a serious brain injury in 2011 during a mass shooting in which she was the intended target.

After Connecticut's General Assembly passed the package of gun laws, and Gov. Dannel P. Malloy, a Democrat, signed it into law, gun-related deaths started to drop. According to the chief medical examiner's office in Connecticut, the number of deaths resulting from firearms — including homicides, suicides and accidents — fell to 164 in 2016, from 226 in 2012.

There is no doubt that there are limits to state and local gun laws. Cities like Chicago and Baltimore, with rigorous gun laws, also have two of the highest murder rates in the country. The black market for illegal guns has thrived in those cities, with gang members and criminals turning to the streets to get firearms.

And the drop in fatal shootings in Connecticut has occurred in the context of a broad, long-term decline in violent crime across the country. Citing F.B.I. statistics, the Pew Research Center reports that violent crime fell 48 percent from 1993 to 2016.

Gun-rights groups say the problem is not the guns, but the individuals using them. They argue that laws alone are no panacea, and that

JESSICA HILL FOR THE NEW YORK TIMES

From left, Mark Barden, the father of the Sandy Hook shooting victim Daniel Barden; Nicole Hockley, the mother of the victim Dylan Hockley; and Gilles Rousseau, the father of the victim Lauren Rousseau, listened last year during a news conference on the steps of the Connecticut Supreme Court. They are plaintiffs in a lawsuit against the companies that made and sold the weapon used in the Sandy Hook massacre.

social issues like mental illness and unemployment must be addressed to help curb gun violence. Some gun advocates have also called for more training and security for those who legally and responsibly maintain guns.

Still, with little appetite in Congress to take on gun control, the debate is playing out at the state level, with Connecticut seen as a model for gun-control advocates.

"Connecticut's laws are among the nation's toughest and homicides are down," Senator Richard Blumenthal, Democrat of Connecticut, said. "Obviously the link is a circumstantial one; cause and effect can't be proven conclusively. But the numbers are all in the right direction. States like Connecticut can help shame Congress into adopting common-sense measures that keep guns out of the hands of dangerous people."

State officials say Connecticut has experienced the fastest drop in violent crime of any state over the last four years. Gun-control advocates say the suspect in Florida, Nikolas Cruz, could not have bought the AR-15-style semiautomatic rifle believed used in the attack, or the high-capacity magazines, in Connecticut.

"We really need to do a better job at making sure we have strong gun laws in every state in the country, because we are losing our most valuable resource, which is our children," said Jeremy I. Stein, the executive director of CT Against Gun Violence, a nonprofit advocacy group.

Even in Connecticut, where parents of the children killed at Sandy Hook met with lawmakers as they debated the legislation, the measures fell short of what gun-control advocates wanted. For example, the laws did not force residents to relinquish existing assault weapons and high-capacity magazines or limit the number of firearms people could own.

At a hearing a month after the Newtown shooting, some speakers talked of the need to hold people accountable. "The problem is not gun laws. The problem is a lack of civility," said Mark Mattioli, whose son James, 6, was killed at Sandy Hook Elementary.

The Giffords Center, which keeps a state-by-state report card, gave Connecticut an A-minus for its gun laws — the same grade given to New York, which moved even more swiftly after Sandy Hook to pass stricter laws. The center ranked Connecticut 46th and New York 48th for their gun death rates, among the five lowest in the United States.

In New York, Gov. Andrew M. Cuomo signed a law a month after the massacre at Sandy Hook that is, in some respects, stricter than the one in Connecticut. The New York law not only bans the sale of assault weapons and imposes universal background checks, it also prohibits both the sale — and possession — of magazines with a capacity of more than 10 rounds. And it requires mental health professionals to alert the authorities about at-risk patients who should not be allowed to buy a firearm. As of Feb. 8, 77,447 people deemed to be dangerously mentally ill had been added to the database.

Avery W. Gardiner, a president of the Brady Campaign to Prevent Gun Violence, said that generally, blue states are, not surprisingly, more likely to regulate guns and require background checks and licensing. Conservative red states either lack gun-safety laws or fail to enforce the ones they have. Her group's strategy includes filing lawsuits to enforce existing safety laws and countering the gun lobby, which uses its muscle in statehouses as well as Congress.

The lobbying has been hard on both sides. According to the nonpartisan National Institute on Money in State Politics, in the past three election cycles the National Rifle Association, the nation's leading gun lobby, spent a total of $10.6 million to support candidates for state office in 25 states. Between 2009 and 2016, at least two-thirds of that spending went to state contests in which the group's chosen candidate won.

"Florida has gone the wrong way since Sandy Hook for sensible laws," Ms. Gardiner said, citing a Florida law that would have restricted doctors from even asking patients about gun safety. The Brady Center sued Florida on the grounds that the law violated the First Amendment's guarantee of free speech, and a year ago a panel of federal judges ruled in the center's favor.

In Connecticut, the question of magazine capacity became emotionally charged as the stricter gun laws were being debated. That is because the Sandy Hook attacker, Adam Lanza, like other mass gunmen, used high-capacity magazines that allowed him to rapidly fire 30 rounds. A group of first graders at Sandy Hook ran past Mr. Lanza, escaping from the hail of bullets when he had to stop and reload.

At a news conference in April 2013, on the day lawmakers announced an agreement on gun control, Nicole Hockley, whose son, Dylan, died at Sandy Hook, said: "We ask ourselves every day — every minute — if those magazines had held 10 rounds, forcing the shooter to reload at least six more times, would our children be alive today?"

Connecticut's sweeping gun laws did, however, require residents who already owned high-capacity magazines and assault rifles to register them with the State Police. Today, the registry lists 52,648 assault weapons. A single resident registered 179 assault weapons, while another registered more than 500,000 magazines exceeding the 10-round limit. Between 2013 and 2017, 248 people were charged with illegally possessing an assault weapon because they either failed to register an existing weapon or had bought a weapon after the law went into effect.

The state also requires that individuals admitted to psychiatric hospitals relinquish their guns, at least temporarily. The State Police is notified of such patients by the Department of Mental Health and Addiction Services, which maintains a database, and ensures that upon discharge, the gun owner turns in the weapon or transfers it to someone eligible for a gun permit. In addition, people who were previously treated in a mental hospital cannot get a permit for up to two years afterward.

The National Shooting Sports Foundation, a lobby group in Newtown, Conn., declined to comment on the impact of Connecticut's gun laws "out of respect for the families, the community and the ongoing law enforcement investigation" in Parkland, Fla. The National Rifle Association did not respond to a request to comment.

Connecticut is also one of a few states with another gun law with some teeth — an "extreme risk protection order." Akin to a restraining order for domestic violence victims, the protection order, which predates Sandy Hook, gives the police the power to temporarily take away an individual's guns if a person makes threats, acts violently, abuses drugs or commits animal cruelty.

In the Florida massacre, the authorities believe that the gunman may have made threatening comments on social media, including one last September — "I'm going to be a professional school shooter" — and had also posted a photo of a bloodied frog.

A study that examined Connecticut's risk protection order found that, from 1999 to 2013, 99 percent of warrants led to the confiscation of at least one gun. In nearly half the cases, the gun owner wound up receiving psychiatric treatment.

Mike Lawlor, the criminal justice adviser to Governor Malloy, said that the law arose from two high-profile shootings in the 1990s by people with severe mental health issues. "When there's no law that's actually been broken, but when there is real evidence that the person is a danger to others, the police need to have an option," he said. "Step one is to get the guns."

Get Out of Facebook and Into the N.R.A.'s Face

OPINION | THOMAS L. FRIEDMAN | FEB. 20, 2018

CAMERON KASKY, a 17-year-old at Marjory Stoneman Douglas High School who survived last week's mass shooting, wrote a beautiful essay for CNN.com that declared: "At the end of the day, the students at my school felt one shared experience — our politicians abandoned us by failing to keep guns out of schools. But this time, my classmates and I are going to hold them to account. This time we are going to pressure them to take action. This time we are going to force them to spend more energy protecting human lives than unborn fetuses."

Cameron, God bless you for that sentiment. But just one piece of respectful advice: If your generation and mine want to get serious about a gun control crusade, we all need to get out of Facebook and into someone's face: the N.R.A.'s.

This fight can't be won on Twitter or Instagram. They do get people into the streets. But social media have created a world of faux activism — "Hey, I tweeted about it" — that the bad guys take advantage of. The N.R.A. is not just in the chat rooms. It's in the cloakrooms of Congress and state legislatures. And it's there with bags of money and votes it uses to reward lawmakers who do its bidding and hurt those who don't.

I loved seeing the 100 students from your high school taking buses Tuesday to Florida's capital to directly press lawmakers. That's a great start. I hope every high school follows.

But, ultimately, nothing will change unless young and old who oppose the N.R.A. run for office, vote, help someone vote, register someone to vote or help fund someone's campaign — so we can threaten the same electoral pain as the National Rifle Association, which, according to PolitiFact, spent $203.2 million between 1998 and 2017 funding its candidates, defeating gun control advocates and lobbying. This is not about persuading people with better ideas. We tried that. It's about generating raw electoral power and pain.

Because most of the G.O.P. members of Congress who do the N.R.A.'s bidding care about only one thing: their jobs. The pay of a typical congressman is $174,000 — and free parking at Reagan National Airport — and they will sell themselves to whoever can generate the votes to enable them to keep both.

Are some Democratic lawmakers cowards, too? You bet. But I can show you plenty who have bucked their party's orthodoxies on education and trade and who insisted that their much-admired colleague Senator Al Franken had to resign over sexual harassment allegations. And most of them have long dared to lose elections to oppose the N.R.A. This is primarily a G.O.P. problem today.

How do we know that? Read the paper or the web. The G.O.P., which claimed to stand for conservative family values, has prostrated itself before the most indecent person to ever occupy the White House — a man who lies as he breathes, smears poor, nonwhite nations and reportedly had sex with a porn star shortly after his wife delivered their son. But G.O.P. lawmakers are mute on this because President Trump energizes their base and ensures their $174,000-a-year jobs and free parking at Reagan National Airport.

This is a party whose evangelicals have been telling us for decades that life is so sacred the G.O.P. must oppose abortion — even in the case of rape, incest or risk to the mother's life. But Republicans won't back common-sense gun laws that would protect fully developed human beings — because the N.R.A. energizes their base and funds their campaigns and ensures their $174,000-a-year jobs and free parking at Reagan National Airport.

This is a party whose "Freedom Caucus" was so obsessed with our rising national debt that it tried to prevent Barack Obama from spending a dime to stimulate our economy after it went deep into recession — but just voted to add $1 trillion to the debt for a corporate tax cut without regard for the burden put on our kids. Republicans did so because Trump energizes their base and ensures that they keep their $174,000-a-year jobs and free parking at Reagan National Airport.

Trying to embarrass them to act on principle is wasted breath. I suspect they're already embarrassed. When these G.O.P. lawmakers are alone at home contemplating the pictures of all these kids gunned down in Florida — thinking about what it'd be like to be one of their parents — plenty of them probably feel filthy for doing the N.R.A.'s bidding.

They know full well that most voters are not asking to scrap the Second Amendment, but for common-sense gun laws that could prevent or reduce more school shootings and would not interfere with any decent Americans' right to own guns for hunting, sports or self-protection.

They know full well that a common-sense banning of all military assault weapons, high-capacity magazines and bump stocks, or mandating universal background checks for gun buyers or to prevent terrorists and the mentally ill from buying guns, would not curb the constitutional right to bear arms.

They know full well that they're in the grip of an N.R.A. cult, whose heart is so frozen, it's content to watch innocent children and adults get gunned down weekly — rather than impose common-sense gun limits. They know all of this — but they suppress it, because they also know if they vote for common-sense gun laws, the N.R.A. will fund their next opponent. Like I said, this is just about raw naked power, and that is what sensible gun control advocates have to generate more of now — in the form of votes and campaign funding. Otherwise nothing changes.

Keep speaking out, Cameron — but never underestimate what some people will do for a $174,000 job and free parking at Reagan National Airport.

I Interned for Senator Rubio. Now I'm Begging Him to Act on Guns.

OPINION | BY SHANA ROSENTHAL | FEB. 20, 2018

DEAR SENATOR RUBIO,

I am writing to you as a former employee of your Tallahassee, Florida office. My sophomore year at Florida State University, I accepted a non-partisan internship at your Tallahassee, Fla. location. As an eager, young Political Science student, I was excited to get my foot in the door of a Senator's office; however, I was dismayed when your staff told me that you probably wouldn't be present for the duration of my internship.

As it turns out, they were right — I worked for your team for five whole months, twenty hours a week, and never once saw you in the office.

As an intern, I was tasked with fielding constituents' calls and writing their comments into a call log, which was sent to you at the end of each week. Supposedly, you used this log to address the needs of constituents, but I am skeptical that you ever actually read through it.

Now, three years later, I am one of those concerned constituents pleading for change from you, our elected Florida official. I am afraid, though, that my pleas for help will fall on the ears of another intern and go no further — but you can prove me wrong by taking action against gun violence.

When I was 19-years-old, FSU — my home away from home — experienced a campus shooting. On November 20, 2015, Myron May approached the Strozier Library on FSU's campus and opened fire on students using a .380-caliber handgun. Three of my fellow colleagues were injured. May was mentally disturbed and consumed by paranoia to a point where he sought to murder people on my campus.

Thankfully, during the shooting I was not at the scene of the crime, but rather, across the street sitting in my dorm. While I studied for my upcoming finals, students were being shot a few yards away from me.

When I was 20-years-old, yet another community I hold close to my heart suffered a mass shooting. On June 12, 2016, Omar Mateen killed 49 people and wounded 58 others using an AR-15 style-rifle at Pulse nightclub in Orlando, Fla. Mateen specifically targeted LGBTQ+ Latinx/ people-of-color that evening.

I was about one mile up the same street from the massacre that night. Again, a blood bath occurred yards away from me and my friends.

Less than 7 months later, tragedy struck while I was visiting home for winter break. January 6, 2017, Esteban Santiago-Ruiz used a Walther PPS 9mm semi-automatic pistol to gun down five individuals and injure six others at Fort Lauderdale-Hollywood International Airport. The Broward County airport my family used to travel our entire lives became a warzone.

Today, I am a 21-year-old college graduate and am writing this with great despair — and even more anger. On February 14, 2018, Nikolas Cruz used an AR-15 style-rifle to murder 17 Marjory Stoneman Douglas High School students and staff, and injured at least 14 more.

I sat in my parents' home, just around the corner from my alma mater, as children were being slaughtered. Once again, I sat in a silo of safety as a bloody massacre literally played out across the street.

I've lived in the serene town of Parkland since I was three-years-old, and attended MSD for four formative years of my life. The hallways where I once shared laughter, curiosity, and hope are now crime scenes. Members of my community have lost their lives. Students and staff of MSD are traumatized. My tight-knit community of loving people is broken.

I am in shock that one of the deadliest mass shootings in American history happened in Parkland, Fla., my hometown — the safest place in Florida.

In my short lifetime, these countless acts of terror have plagued communities throughout the United States with unimaginable grief, and it is time for this pattern to stop. I will no longer feel helpless nor sit idly by while these atrocities occur.

I will not accept mass shootings as the norm.

It is YOUR responsibility as our elected official to pass laws that protect your constituents. This isn't about party politics — this is about human lives. I am begging you to implement a systematic plan that will end the mass shooting epidemic in Florida and beyond, starting with:

- Stricter gun licensing
- Recognizing gun violence as a public health issue
- Funding research on gun violence and gun violence prevention
- Extensive background checks for gun purchases
- Close loopholes in gun purchasing (i.e. gun shows)
- Implementing a buffer period between purchasing a rifle and taking it home

It is shameful that I have to write this and beg you to do SOMETHING.

I hope you have read my letter free from the influence of wealthy lobbyists who may impede your senatorial judgment. I hope you read this letter at all.

Respectfully, your former intern and concerned Parkland citizen,
Shana Miranda Rosenthal

SHANA ROSENTHAL (@SHANAMROSENTHAL) IS A RECENT GRADUATE OF FLORIDA STATE UNIVERSITY, WHERE SHE STUDIED POLITICAL SCIENCE AND COMMUNICATIONS.

Dear National Rifle Association: We Won't Let You Win. From, Teenagers.

OPINION | BY DARCY SCHLEIFSTEIN, ZACHARY DOUGHERTY AND
SARAH EMILY BAUM | MARCH 13, 2018

THE KILLINGS of 17 people at Marjory Stoneman Douglas High School in Florida may be the massacre that finally gets federal and state governments to enact common-sense gun control laws. That should have happened after Columbine. It should have happened after Virginia Tech. It should have happened after Sandy Hook. But it didn't.

The Stoneman Douglas shooting is where our generation draws a line. Our parents and grandparents did not succeed in ensuring our safety at school. So we must do it ourselves.

We are Generation Z, the generation after millennials. We outnumber them by nearly one million and may be the largest cohort of future American spenders since the baby boomers. We have more than $30 billion in spending power and wield enormous influence in family spending. Our spending power will only increase as we begin to earn our own wages.

We will flex our muscles at the ballot box, too. Many high school seniors will cast their first ballots this November, and in 2020, a majority of today's high school students will most likely be able to vote in their first presidential election. And we will not forget the elected officials who turned their backs on their duty to protect children.

Let us remind politicians like Donald Trump, Paul Ryan and Mitch McConnell who accept donations from the National Rifle Association and oppose efforts to restrict gun purchases that we are the future leaders and voters of this country. Let us remind corporations like FedEx that provide discounts to N.R.A. members that we are their future customers.

The Stoneman Douglas students who began speaking out after the killings last month have better articulated the need for common-sense gun control laws and school safety than our elders ever have. But those students cannot do it alone. We as a generation must band together behind them, just as Alexander Hamilton, James Madison, Thomas Jefferson and others stood behind George Washington and fought to create this great country.

We applaud many of the elected officials who have said they will work to reduce gun violence in their states. We hope Gov. Phil Murphy of New Jersey, our home state, will work with us and other advocates to do the same. We also support companies like Dick's Sporting Goods, Avis Budget Group, Hertz, Delta, United and Walmart, which have stood behind the principles of the March for Our Lives movement and either cut ties with the N.R.A. or changed their policies on firearms sales.

On March 24, hundreds of thousands of children and teenagers nationwide will participate in March for Our Lives. We are among the 19 students helping organize New Jersey's march, which will take place in Newark, a city with far too much gun violence. We implore students, their parents, teachers, school administrators, religious leaders, corporate executives and elected officials across the country to join any march, no matter where they are, and fight to make our schools safe.

March for Our Lives is not just one day. It represents the official start of when we all must stand with the Stoneman Douglas students and say, "Never again." This isn't about being aligned with one political party or another. This is about protecting this nation's children, whether they are related to you by blood, or whether they are children you have taught or nurtured.

We are the future of this country, yet we can no longer assume that we are safe from mass shootings in our schools. Nor can we assume our elders will protect us. Instead, we have to work ourselves to end senseless killing, not just for our sakes, but for the sakes of future generations of Americans.

DARCY SCHLEIFSTEIN IS A SOPHOMORE AT RANDOLPH HIGH SCHOOL, **ZACHARY DOUGHERTY** IS A JUNIOR AT TOMS RIVER NORTH HIGH SCHOOL AND **SARAH EMILY BAUM** IS A SENIOR AT MARLBORO HIGH SCHOOL, ALL IN NEW JERSEY.

Florida Students Began With Optimism. Then They Spoke to Lawmakers.

BY JULIE TURKEWITZ | FEB. 21, 2018

TALLAHASSEE — The morning began with optimism. It did not last long.

On Wednesday, students from Marjory Stoneman Douglas High School in Parkland awoke to an overcast sky. They had slept on green cots in the Tallahassee civic center, and it had been a long, cold night. Some agreed that their blankets had smelled strangely like bacon. Many had been up past 3 a.m., researching lawmakers and editing speeches. They had runny eggs, home fries — and bacon — for breakfast.

Then, a week after a shooting rampage killed 17 at their high school, the students headed for the capitol, marching together up a hill, past a statue of leaping dolphins. They had come to urge lawmakers to impose new restrictions on guns, including a ban on the sale of military-style firearms like the AR-15 used in the rampage at their school. A former student, Nikolas Cruz, has been charged in the slayings.

As the students walked to the capitol, Rosio Briones, 17, was quiet. "I don't know how to put my thoughts into words," she said. "This still feels so surreal to me."

But another student, Olivia Feller, 16, stood with Anthony Lopez, 16, and ran through a list of state legislators: who supported what, who they might be able to sway. "We are ready," she said. "Sleep deprived but ready."

Outside the capitol, Senator Aaron Bean, a Republican, was rushing into the building.

How did he feel about the student visit? a reporter asked.

"Angst," he said. "I just — there is so much emotion. I'm really really sad. It's a very sad situation. Kids shouldn't have to worry about that. It's already tough enough being a teenager, without worrying about things like that."

Did he plan to vote in favor of any bills that would do anything about that?

"You know, I think it's too early to say."

Why?

"It's just too early to say."

Inside, the students divided into groups of 10. Senator Lauren Book, a Democrat, had helped the students arrange meetings with lawmakers in both parties, and the groups were supposed to meet with some 70 elected officials.

Group Six crammed into the elevator with two parent chaperones. They met with Representative Patricia H. Williams, a Democrat, and Senator Debbie Mayfield, a Republican. Ms. Mayfield said that changes were needed, perhaps including raising the minimum age to buy powerful weapons, but she rebuffed criticism from a student, Daniel Bishop, 16, that such a change would not actually prevent deaths.

"We can't stop crazies," she told the group.

Afterward, Amanda De La Cruz, 16, looked distraught. "I want the ban on semiautomatic weapons," she said. "I don't care about the crazies."

Then they headed to the House floor, where the powerful speaker of the House, Richard Corcoran, a Republican, had agreed to take their questions.

Standing at the front of the chamber, he promised to unveil what he said would be the most sweeping gun reform package in the nation's history by Thursday or Friday.

Then a 16-year-old student named Alondra Gittelson raised her hand.

"I just want to know why such a destructive gun is accessible to the public — why that gun, the AR-15, that did so much damage, how is an individual in society able to acquire such a gun?"

Mr. Corcoran responded that he would not be in favor of banning weapons like the one used in the attack on the students.

"I think that if you look, it's widely used in multiple different hunting scenarios," he said. "I know people who go out and they'll do boar hunts and they'll use them."

He continued: "You can disagree, but what I tell my kids — and being in elected office, you have to be very, very, very careful how much authority and power you bring to government. The greatest atrocities known to mankind have been committed by governments."

"I understand your question," he added. "And we'll look at it, but I'll just be honest with you: Me personally I don't believe that's the solution."

Afterward, Ms. Gittelson observed that Mr. Corcoran had said exactly what her stepfather had predicted he would say.

Around noon, hundreds of people converged on the capitol in support of the Stoneman Douglas students. Then, in the afternoon, the tone inside the capitol changed, as protesters flooded the building.

The morning had been filled with impassioned but respectful conversation between the Stoneman Douglas students and lawmakers. But as the day wore on, college students and others packed the hallways carrying signs and boxes of petitions.

On one floor, they crowded the doorway of the office of Gov. Rick Scott, shouting "Shame! Shame! Shame!" On an upper floor, they gathered outside Mr. Corcoran's office: "Face us down! Face us down! Face us down!"

As the students pressed lawmakers in Tallahassee, cries for stricter gun control measures swelled on sidewalks and football fields around the country.

Back in South Florida, students formed an enormous heart on an athletic field at Coral Springs High School and then walked to Stoneman Douglas High School, about five miles away, where more than 1,000 students gathered.

"Seventeen lives are more important than gun rights," said Christopher Lormeus, 18, who had walked from Coconut Creek High School, six miles away.

Near Tampa, thousands of students left their classrooms and stood silently for 17 minutes, according to The Tampa Bay Times.

The protests stretched far beyond Florida. In Montgomery County, Md., students left their high schools, walked to the Metro, and rallied in front of the Capitol, holding signs with slogans like, "Protect kids not guns."

They walked out of Simon Kenton High School in Kentucky, according to the Enquirer, chanting "never again," and filed out of Mesa High School in Arizona, hoping to support the Parkland students. "This is our mark in history," one student said, to whoops and cheers.

But at Needville High School, about an hour outside Houston, administrators threatened any student who protested during school hours with a three-day suspension.

"Life is all about choices and every choice has a consequence whether it be positive or negative," Curtis Rhodes, the superintendent, said in a statement posted on Facebook. "We will discipline no matter if it is one, 50, or 500 students involved."

Outspoken and Precocious, Florida Students Struggle With Loss When the Cameras Turn Off

BY JACK HEALY | FEB. 25, 2018

Even as they raise millions of dollars and plan nationwide rallies to stop gun violence, students at Marjory Stoneman Douglas High School struggle with nightmares.

PARKLAND, FLA. — After a gunman turned their high school into a sprawling crime scene last week, three freshman friends leapt into the student movement for tougher gun laws. They rode a bus to the State Capitol and chased down lawmakers. They vowed to march on Washington. They shouted and waved signs saying "Protect Kids" and "Stop Killing the Future."

But at night, in the blackness that recalls the dark classroom where she hid as a gunman murdered her classmates, Samara Barrack, 15, cannot stop thinking about that afternoon, when she fled through a blood-covered hallway. Samantha Deitsch, also 15, grieves a friend from journalism class. Aria Siccone, 14, who walked past the bodies of students from her last-period study hall, feels nothing sometimes. Just numbness.

"I keep having flashbacks," Samara said. "There's times I want to cry and can't. There's times I want to have fun and am hysterical."

This is the reality that confronts students at Marjory Stoneman Douglas High School when the cameras turn off and the day's rallies are over. They have won praise for their strength and eloquence on the world's stage. But even as they raise millions of dollars and plan nationwide rallies, parse the details of assault-weapons laws and spar with politicians and conservative critics, the young survivors of the massacre are struggling with the loss of their friends and educators, and the nightmares that flood back in moments of stillness.

Michele Barrack hugged her daughter Samara, a freshman at Marjory Stoneman Douglas High School in Parkland, Fla., where a gunman killed 17 this month.

And Parkland, once named Florida's safest city by a home-security group, is today a place carved open by rage, grief and questions about whether any child, anywhere, can ever be safe from a spray of bullets.

It is a place where friends now attend counseling together, where parents worry how their children will head to campus when classes resume on Wednesday. It is a place where strangers hug one another in a memorial park that bears crosses and Stars of David for the 17 victims, where others break down as they lay flowers at the fence surrounding M.S.D., as the school is known.

"It's ripped the rug out because we're such a close-knit community," the Parkland mayor, Christine Hunschofsky, said.

The Spanish-tiled houses and fairway-view homes of subdivisions named Heron Bay and Water's Edge are filled with families who chose Parkland for its schools and safety. It draws families from Florida and beyond, and the parental contact lists for school groups are filled with area codes from Boston, New Jersey, New York and Philadelphia. Children ride their bikes to community pools and grow up listening to alligators chortle at night. The Parkland bubble, people call it.

"It's beautiful and brand-new, and has been since I've gotten here," said Sara Giovanello, a senior whose family moved from Long Island, N.Y., when she was 9. "I feel like they're building something more every day."

And to teachers and parents, Stoneman Douglas High School, with its rank of 50th in the state by U.S. News and World Report and its 94 percent graduation rate, was its crown jewel. It is a vast campus of 3,000 students whose schedules overflow with extracurricular activities: sports, speech, drama, literary clubs, a gay-straight alliance, poetry slams, television production, a marching band and more.

Caitlyn Rosenblatt, 16, who grew up here, put it like this: "The day I was born, my parents knew I was going to Stoneman Douglas."

Before the shooting, arguments over gun control were hashed out in debate classes. Meditations on isolation and death were composed for speech tournaments. A congressman who represents the heavily

Barbara Ramaley, a crossing guard at Stoneman Douglas, visited a memorial to those killed in the shooting.

Democratic area addressed students at the invitation of the politics club. Student mental-health issues were discussed in The Eagle Eye, the school newspaper.

Now, as students brace themselves to return to classes this week, evenings at friends' houses have turned into organizing meetings. Group phone chats that once revolved around physics problems and A.P. Literature sonnets are now filled with plans for rallies, vigils and news about legislation and gun politics. Their personal social media accounts are now hugely popular springboards for action, such as the student journalist David Hogg's call for a boycott of Florida's spring break season if lawmakers do not tighten gun laws.

Students said that activism has helped them grieve, and wrought some purpose from the senseless killings of their friends. Ashley Turner, a senior, made plans to donate blood, and said she thought enduring all of this would make her stronger.

But she still wakes in the middle of the night, her heart pounding, her body beaded with sweat.

"I attended five funerals," she said. "There are times where I just want to cry. There are times when I feel nothing. There are times where I feel angry and just want to snap at people."

Jack Haimowitz, 18, now rarely falls asleep before 1 a.m., so every night, he chooses three friends from his phone contacts and calls to check in. Are you eating? Are you O.K.? Some scroll through their phones for hours, scared to sleep, Jack said. Others feel helpless or cry when he calls.

He thinks all the time about his friend Joaquin Oliver — Guac to friends — who loved football and basketball. Jack sometimes thumbs through the text messages he sent Joaquin after the shots were fired, asking where he was, whether he was injured, whether the rumors were true, begging for a reply.

Jack Haimowitz, a senior at Stoneman Douglas, watched himself read a letter to his friend Joaquin Oliver, who was killed in the shooting, on the "Dr. Phil" show.

Even tiny things can reanimate what some students simply call "the event." Lea Serrano, 14, who heard the shooting from just a few feet away, flinched a day later when her father handed her an object wrapped in black. It was simply a bag with headphones inside. A set of keys jangling when she and her family were at a seafood restaurant prompted fears that someone would shoot her.

"This stuff comes in waves," she said.

But the world was calm for the moment in Samara Barrack's backyard, the pool washing a soft blue light over the three friends who bounced and laughed on a trampoline. They had been leaning on one another more than ever since the shooting, sleeping over and texting and sharing memories of running the mile with Alaina Petty, killed at 14, or mimicking people in viral videos with Jaime Guttenberg, killed at 14.

"We can be silly together," Samara said.

Aria, who witnessed part of the shooting through the window of her classroom door, has played and replayed those minutes in her head,

JUSTIN GILLILAND FOR THE NEW YORK TIMES

From left, Aria Siccone, Samantha Deitsch and Samara Barrack at Ms. Barrack's home in Parkland. The three students have been leaning on one another after the shooting, sleeping over and sharing memories.

trying to reconstruct what she saw and square it against reports on the news. She gets upset when she hears a detail that she insists is wrong. She knows, she says. She was there.

"I don't feel anything, and it's really weird," Aria said. "I can't cry anymore. Or feel things."

They talked about being worried about their friends, how some seemed O.K. and others "not O.K." They said they hoped to nudge a few toward counseling.

Inside, the girls' parents wondered what "O.K." meant, now and in the future. They were awed by how their children had responded to the shooting by researching gun laws and trying to forge change. But they worried about how their children were processing the trauma and grief, and how they could ever reclaim their childhoods.

"They had to grow up, just like that," Samantha's father, Rik Deitsch, said.

"I don't know if we've seen the worst," said Steven Siccone, Aria's father. "I think it's still to come."

"They're happy when they're with each other," Samara's mother, Michele Barrack, said.

The girls went upstairs to Samara's room, where they flopped onto her bed and cuddled a 6-week-old puppy that Samantha's parents had bought after the shooting. They named it Misty, to echo M.S.D., and cooed at it and encouraged it to waddle across the floor.

Then Samara's sixth-grade sister offered a suggestion: "Let's all talk about our fears."

Aria said hers was the doctor's office: "Getting shots."

"Mine is yawning and your jaw getting stuck," Samantha said.

Samara thought for a moment.

"Mine is being trapped in a room and having something close in on you."

JULIE TURKEWITZ AND PATRICIA MAZZEI CONTRIBUTED REPORTING.

Major Shootings Led to Tougher Gun Laws, but to What End?

BY LINDA QIU AND JUSTIN BANK | FEB. 23, 2018

WASHINGTON — Since last week's deadly shooting at a high school in Parkland, Fla., a pitched national conversation about gun policy has dominated town hall meetings, a White House summit meeting, the annual Conservative Political Action Conference and the never-ending stream of social media feeds.

Below is a brief review of several laws governing guns in the United States and how effective those policies have been in curbing violence.

HIGH-PROFILE SHOOTINGS PROMPTED SEVERAL MAJOR FEDERAL GUN LAWS.

Some of the toughest laws that regulate the production, distribution and use of firearms in the United States were passed after major acts of violence.

• The National Firearms Act of 1934 was signed by President Franklin D. Roosevelt after high-profile gangland crimes, including the St. Valentine's Day Massacre in 1929 that killed seven in Chicago. The law imposed a $200 tax on transfers of machine guns, short-barrel rifles and shotguns, and it required gun owners to register those weapons.

At the time, the tax was "considered quite severe and adequate" to discourage or eliminate sales of those guns, according to the Bureau of Alcohol, Tobacco, Firearms and Explosives. It still stands at $200 — even though its current value, after adjusting for inflation, would come to about $3,700.

• The Gun Control Act of 1968 was passed after the assassinations of President John F. Kennedy, the Rev. Dr. Martin Luther King Jr. and Robert F. Kennedy. It banned interstate mail orders of all firearms, interstate handgun sales and weapons with no "sporting purpose." It prohibited the sale of firearms to minors, felons, fugitives, drug addicts and those committed to a mental institution. And it required gun manufacturers and dealers to be licensed and maintain records of sales.

• After an intense lobbying effort by gun advocates, the Firearms Owners' Protection Act of 1986 lifted some of those restrictions. The 1986 law allowed dealers to sell rifles and shotguns through the mail, and it limited federal inspections of gun dealers. It also prohibited the sale of machine guns manufactured after May 19, 1986.

• The Brady Handgun Violence Prevention Act of 1993 further amended the 1968 law: It required gun purchasers not already licensed to possess a firearm to undergo background checks when buying from sellers licensed by the federal government. However, private transactions were exempted, creating the so-called gun-show loophole.

• The Violent Crime Control and Law Enforcement Act of 1994 banned the possession, transfer or domestic manufacturing of some semiautomatic assault weapons for 10 years. Known as the Federal Assault Weapons Ban, it expired in 2004, despite efforts by gun control advocates to extend it.

• In 2008, Congress passed the NICS Improvement Amendments Act after a shooting at Virginia Tech a year earlier had killed 33. The law created a series of incentives and systems — but not requirements — for states to share information with the federal government about people who have been disqualified from obtaining guns.

HERE'S WHAT STATES HAVE DONE.

Eight states have enacted some kind of ban on assault weapons. Two other states regulate military-grade firearms. State gun laws are tracked, in detail, by the Giffords Law Center to Prevent Gun Violence, which lobbies for gun control.

According to the law center, states with the strictest gun control measures have the lowest rates of gun-related deaths. Those states include California, Connecticut, New Jersey and New York. Conversely, states that do not aggressively regulate guns — like Alabama, Alaska and Louisiana — have the highest.

Still, as Lisa Foderaro and Kristin Hussey have reported for The New York Times, "Cities like Chicago and Baltimore, with rigorous gun laws, also have two of the highest murder rates in the country. The black market for illegal guns has thrived in those cities, with gang members and criminals turning to the streets to get firearms."

Some state gun control laws have come under court review. In one prominent case, the Supreme Court limited gun control efforts in its 2009 ruling District of Columbia v. Heller.

Since then, however, the United States' highest court has opted to not consider other Second Amendment cases, including in 2016, when it declined to hear challenges to bans on assault weapons in Connecticut and New York. Those state laws were passed after 20 first graders and six adults were killed in a mass shooting at Sandy Hook Elementary School in Newtown, Conn.

In choosing to not hear those cases, "the justices have given at least tacit approval to broad gun control laws in states and localities that choose to enact them," wrote Adam Liptak, the legal affairs correspondent for The Times.

BUT TO WHAT EFFECT?

It's difficult to directly link declines in crime or gun violence to any specific law, given the limited scope and loopholes in each one, according to experts and research.

The National Rifle Association has "successfully built in ineffectiveness" to gun control legislation, said Adam Winkler, a law professor at the University of California, Los Angeles, and the author of "Gunfight: The Battle Over the Right to Bear Arms in America."

"Part of the story is that the N.R.A. fights tooth and nail against any policy," Mr. Winkler said. "The laws that result are much less ambitious in their goals."

The gun control laws had some effect. The 1934 restrictions curbed access to machine guns; crimes with those types of fully automatic firearms have essentially dried up since the era of Al Capone. The 1968 prohibitions on who can own a weapon, and requirements for licensing dealers, are still in place.

The 1994 ban on assault weapons has become a particular and recent subject of intense debate. The N.R.A. has cited a 2004 analysis funded by the Justice Department to argue that the "ban could not be credited with any reduction in crime."

On the other hand, Senator Dianne Feinstein, Democrat of California, has claimed in a Twitter post that "the number of gun massacres fell by 37%" while the ban was in place.

Christopher Koper, a professor at George Mason University in Fairfax, Va., and the lead author of the study that is cited by the N.R.A., has repeatedly said that the ban had mixed effects and final results would not be immediately evident.

"My work is often cited in misleading ways that don't give the full picture," Mr. Koper said Thursday in an email. "These laws can modestly reduce shootings overall" and reduce the number and severity of mass shootings.

Ms. Feinstein's claim that the ban drastically reduced gun massacres comes from analysis by Louis Klarevas, a lecturer at the University of Massachusetts Boston. But Mr. Winkler noted that most mass shootings are committed with a handgun, not a military-grade assault weapon.

"There's no anti-mass shooting law to test," said Charles Branas, the chairman of the epidemiology department at the School of Public Health at Columbia University in New York. "In terms of all of these instances, not just mass shootings, we need the politicians to create more laws to test."

'We Should Not Have This in Common': Santa Fe and Parkland Students React to Shooting

BY NIRAJ CHOKSHI AND AUDRA D. S. BURCH | MAY 18, 2018

THE MASS SHOOTING at a Texas school on Friday introduced a new set of high school students to a pain all too familiar to their peers in Parkland, Fla.

In the hours after the attack, students at both schools — Santa Fe High School in Texas and Marjory Stoneman Douglas High School in Florida — voiced their grief, support and frustration over the violent attack.

To Paige Curry, a student at the Texas school, Friday's tragedy was unsurprising.

"I was thinking it was going to happen eventually, it's been happening everywhere," she said in an interview with KPRC, a local television station.

Kaitlyn Jesionowski, a survivor of that shooting, in which 17 people were killed, first saw news of the Friday attack on Twitter on what was the last day of school for seniors at Marjory Stoneman Douglas. For Ms. Jesionowski, it all came rushing back: the fear, the anxiety, the stress. "I started replaying what happened to us in my head, over and over."

Nikolas Cruz, who has confessed to the Parkland shooting, opened fire in her Holocaust class on the afternoon of Valentine's Day, killing two students and injuring four others, she said. "This has been so hard because all the emotions come back," she said, adding that she was rushing home from school to be with her family.

Samantha Grady, 17, a Parkland classmate who was grazed in the back, learned about the Texas school shooting in a group chat during her study hall period. She stared at the phone. "It's surreal for me, I can only imagine what they are feeling, the fear they experienced having gone through the same thing," she said. "Honestly, I am flabbergasted."

Dakota Shrader, a student at Santa Fe High School, was stunned, too.

"Honestly, I just had the thought in my head that somebody was going to come up behind me and hurt me, shoot me, kill me. I'm still jumpy from it," Ms. Shrader, 16, said in an interview. "I don't know who to trust anymore, at all."

"This should be our safe place," she added.

Many of the students who survived the Parkland shooting agreed.

"WE SHOULD NOT HAVE THIS IN COMMON," Liz Stout, a senior at the school, said on Twitter, linking to a video of Ms. Shrader.

"Today is my last day of school at Marjory Stoneman Douglas High and I find out there's been a shooting in Texas at Santa Fe High School," she wrote on Twitter. "My heart aches for them."

"We are fighting for you," David Hogg, another of the Parkland students, said in a tweet.

Others expressed anger and frustration over what they expected would be a feckless response from politicians and the news media, along with what they predicted would be aggressive pushback from gun rights supporters.

"Prepare to watch the NRA boast about getting higher donations," one Parkland student, Cameron Kasky, said on Twitter. "Prepare to see students rise up and be called 'civil terrorists' and crisis actors. Prepare for the right-wing media to attack the survivors."

Many of them criticized the calls for "thoughts and prayers" that are routinely offered up after such tragedies.

And Fred Guttenberg, whose daughter Jaime was killed in the Valentine's Day shooting in Parkland, said the Texas attack simply underscored the need for swifter action.

"My heart is so heavy for the students of Santa Fe High School," Jaclyn Corin, a Parkland student, said on Twitter. "It's an all too familiar feeling no one should have to experience. I am so sorry this epidemic touched your town — Parkland will stand with you now and forever."

Glossary

active gunman Person in the process of attacking a school or other public location with a firearm.

advocate To argue for a particular outcome or point of view; usually refers to a call for change or justice.

autopsy Examination of a dead body by a medical examiner or doctor for evidence and causes of death.

condolences An empathetic statement offered to someone when a close friend or family member has died.

dissent Disagreement with a policy or authority.

ideology A framework for understanding the world; usually refers to a set of political beliefs.

ostracize To exclude someone from social groups.

outcast Someone who is excluded and who operates on the margins of a society.

person of interest Law enforcement term referring to someone who the police believe may be involved in a crime, but is not yet a confirmed suspect.

rampage Intense, sustained violence.

Second Amendment An amendment to the U.S. Constitution adopted on Dec. 15, 1791 that refers to the "right of the people to keep and bear arms".

trauma Psychological harm caused by experiencing or witnessing a violent event.

Media Literacy Terms

"Media literacy" refers to the ability to access, understand, critically assess and create media. The following terms are important components of media literacy, and they will help you critically engage with the articles in this title.

angle The aspect of a news story that a journalist focuses on and develops.

attribution The method by which a source is identified or by which facts and information are assigned to the person who provided them.

balance Principle of journalism that both perspectives of an argument should be presented in a fair way.

bias A disposition of prejudice in favor of a certain idea, person, or perspective.

byline Name of the writer, usually placed between the headline and the story.

chronological order Method of writing a story presenting the details of the story in the order in which they occurred.

credibility The quality of being trustworthy and believable, said of a journalistic source.

editorial Article of opinion or interpretation.

feature story Article designed to entertain as well as to inform. headline Type, usually 18 point or larger, used to introduce a story.

human interest story Type of story that focuses on individuals and how events or issues affect their life, generally offering a sense of relatability to the reader.

impartiality Principle of journalism that a story should not reflect a journalist's bias and should contain balance.

intention The motive or reason behind something, such as the publication of a news story.

interview story Type of story in which the facts are gathered primarily by interviewing another person or persons.

inverted pyramid Method of writing a story using facts in order of importance, beginning with a lead and then gradually adding paragraphs in order of relevance from most interesting to least interesting.

motive The reason behind something, such as the publication of a news story or a source's perspective on an issue.

news story An article or style of expository writing that reports news, generally in a straightforward fashion and without editorial comment.

op-ed An opinion piece that reflects a prominent journalist's opinion on topic of interest.

paraphrase The summary of an individual's words, with attribution, rather than a direct quotation of their exact words.

quotation The use of an individual's exact words indicated by the use of quotation marks and proper attribution.

reliability The quality of being dependable and accurate, said of a journalistic source.

rhetorical device Technique in writing intending to persuade the reader or communicate a message from a certain perspective.

tone A manner of expression in writing or speech.

Media Literacy Questions

1. Identify the various sources cited in the article "Florida Students Began With Optimism. Then They Spoke to Lawmakers." (on page 195). How does the journalist attribute information to each of these sources in their article? How effective are their attributions in helping the reader identify their sources?

2. Compare the headlines of "Florida Students Began With Optimism. Then They Spoke to Lawmakers." (on page 194) and "I Interned for Senator Rubio. Now I'm Begging Him to Act on Guns." (on page 190). Which is a more compelling headline, and why? How could the less compelling headline be changed to draw better the reader's interest?

3. What type of story is "Should Teachers Carry Guns? Are Metal Detectors Helpful? What Experts Say" (on page 144)? Can you identify another article in this collection that is the same type of story?

4. The article "Get Out of Facebook and Into the N.R.A.'s Face" (on page 187) is an example of an op-ed. Identify how Thomas L. Friedman's attitude, tone and bias help convey their opinion on the topic.

5. What is the intention of the article "Don't Let My Classmates' Deaths Be in Vain" (on page 167)? How effectively does it achieve its intended purpose?

6. What is the intention of the article "The Names and Faces of the Florida School Shooting Victims" (on page 87)? How effectively does it achieve its intended purpose?

7. Analyze the authors' bias in "Reporting on a Mass Shooting, Again" (on page 94) and "'How Did This Happen?': Grief and Fury After Florida Shooting" (on page 97). Do you think one journalist is more biased in his reporting than the other? If so, why do you think so?

8. Does Erica L. Green demonstrate the journalistic principle of impartiality in their article "Trump Finds Unlikely Culprit in School Shootings: Obama Discipline Policies" (on page 138)? If so, how did they do so? If not, what could they have included to make their article more impartial?

9. What type of story is "Nation's Pain Is Renewed, and Difficult Questions Are Asked Once More" (on page 78)? Can you identify another article in this collection that is the same type of story?

10. Identify the various sources cited in the article "Should Teachers Carry Guns? Are Metal Detectors Helpful? What Experts Say" (on page 144). How does the journalist attribute information to each of these sources in their article? How effective are their attributions in helping the reader identify their sources?

11. Identify each of the sources in "Major Shootings Led to Tougher Gun Laws, but to What End?" (on page 206) as a primary source or a secondary source. Evaluate the reliability and credibility of each source. How does your evaluation of each source change your perspective on this article?

12. In "Columbine Shocked the Nation. Now, Mass Shootings Are Less Surprising." (on page 52), Maggie Astor directly quotes Arthur Evans, chief executive of the American Psychological Association. What are the strengths of the use of a direct quote as opposed to a paraphrase? What are its weaknesses?

Citations

All citations in this list are formatted according to the Modern Language Association's (MLA) style guide.

BOOK CITATION

NEW YORK TIMES EDITORIAL STAFF, THE. *School Shootings: How Can We Stop Them?*. New York: New York Times Educational Publishing, 2019.

ARTICLE CITATIONS

ABT, CARSON. "My Teachers at Marjory Stoneman Douglas Saved Lives." *The New York Times*, 26 Feb. 2018, https://www.nytimes.com/2018/02/26/opinion/florida-guns-training-trump.html.

APPLEBOME, PETER, AND MICHAEL WILSON. "'Who Would Do This to Our Poor Little Babies.'" *The New York Times*, 14 Dec. 2012, https://www.nytimes.com/2012/12/15/nyregion/witnesses-recall-deadly-shooting-sandy-hook-newtown-connecticut.html.

ASTOR, MAGGIE. "Columbine Shocked the Nation. Now, Mass Shootings Are Less Surprising." *The New York Times*, 10 Nov. 2017, https://www.nytimes.com/2017/11/10/us/columbine-texas-mass-shooting.html.

ASTOR, MAGGIE. "Florida Legislator's Aide Is Fired After He Calls Parkland Students 'Actors.'" *The New York Times*, 20 Feb. 2018, https://www.nytimes.com/2018/02/20/us/florida-shooting-benjamin-kelly-actors.html.

BARRON, JAMES. "Children in Connecticut School Were All Shot Multiple Times." *The New York Times*, 15 Dec. 2012, https://www.nytimes.com/2012/12/16/nyregion/gunman-kills-20-children-at-school-in-connecticut-28-dead-in-all.html.

BARRON, JAMES. "Gunman Kills 20 Schoolchildren in Connecticut." *The New York Times*, 14 Dec. 2012, https://www.nytimes.com/2012/12/15/nyregion/shooting-reported-at-connecticut-elementary-school.html.

BIDGOOD, JESS. "The Names and Faces of the Florida School Shooting Victims." *The New York Times*, 15 Feb. 2018, https://www.nytimes.com/2018/

02/15/us/florida-school-victims.html.

BLACK, MICHAEL IAN. "The Boys Are Not All Right." *The New York Times*, 21 Feb. 2018, https://www.nytimes.com/2018/02/21/opinion/boys-violence -shootings-guns.html.

BLINDER, ALAN, ET AL. "In School Shooting's Painful Aftermath, Sheriff Faces Questions Over Police Response." *The New York Times*, 21 Feb. 2018, https://www.nytimes.com/2018/02/21/us/police-security-florida-shooting .html.

BROOKE, JAMES. "Terror in Littleton: The Overview; 2 Students in Colorado School Said to Gun down as Many as 23 and Kill Themselves in a Siege." *The New York Times*, 21 Apr. 1999, https://www.nytimes.com/1999/04/21/ us/terror-littleton-overview-2-students-colorado-school-said-gun-down -many-23-kill.html.

BROOKS, DAVID. "The Columbine Killers." *The New York Times*, 24 Apr. 2004, https://www.nytimes.com/2004/04/24/opinion/the-columbine-killers.html.

BURCH, AUDRA D. S., NICK MADIGAN, ET AL. "As Victims Are Mourned in Florida, a Search for Solace, and Action." *The New York Times*, 18 Feb. 2018, https:// www.nytimes.com/2018/02/18/us/florida-shooting-funeral-mourning.html.

BURCH, AUDRA D. S., PATRICIA MAZZEI, ET AL. "A 'Mass Shooting Generation' Cries Out for Change." *The New York Times*, 16 Feb. 2018, https://www .nytimes.com/2018/02/16/us/columbine-mass-shootings.html.

BURCH, AUDRA D. S., AND PATRICIA MAZZEI. "As Shots Ring Out, a Student Texts: 'If I Don't Make It, I Love You.'" *The New York Times*, 14 Feb. 2018, https://www.nytimes.com/2018/02/14/us/florida-school-shooting-scene .html.

CAREY, BENEDICT. "When the Group Is Wise." *The New York Times*, 22 Apr. 2007, https://www.nytimes.com/2007/04/22/weekinreview/22carey.html.

DAVIS, JULIE HIRSCHFELD. "Parents and Students Plead With Trump: 'How Many Children Have to Get Shot?'" *The New York Times*, 21 Feb. 2018, https://www.nytimes.com/2018/02/21/us/politics/trump-guns-school -shooting.html.

DEWAN, SHAILA, AND ARIEL SABAR. "At Virginia Tech, Remembering While Moving On." *The New York Times*, 20 Aug. 2007, https://www.nytimes .com/2007/08/20/us/20vatech.html.

DUNLAP, DAVID W. "1966 | 'The Time Has Come for Action.' " *The New York Times*, 5 Oct. 2017, https://www.nytimes.com/2017/10/05/insider/1966-the -time-has-come-for-action.html.

DWYER, JIM. "Running and Hoping to Find a Child Safe." *The New York Times*, 14 Dec. 2012, https://www.nytimes.com/2012/12/15/nyregion/after -newtown-shooting-running-and-hoping-to-find-a-child-safe.html.

FODERARO, LISA W. "In Wake of Florida Massacre, Gun Control Advocates Look to Connecticut." *The New York Times*, 17 Feb. 2018, https://www .nytimes.com/2018/02/17/nyregion/florida-shooting-parkland-gun-control -connecticut.html.

FRIEDMAN, THOMAS L. "Get Out of Facebook and Into the N.R.A.'s Face." *The New York Times*, 20 Feb. 2018, https://www.nytimes.com/2018/02/20/ opinion/get-out-of-facebook-and-into-the-nras-face.html.

GLABERSON, WILLIAM. "Nation's Pain Is Renewed, and Difficult Questions Are Asked Once More." *The New York Times*, 14 Dec. 2012, https://www .nytimes.com/2012/12/15/nyregion/sandy-hook-shooting-forces -re-examination-of-tough-questions.html.

GOODE, ERICA. "The Things We Know About School Shooters." *The New York Times*, 15 Feb. 2018, https://www.nytimes.com/2018/02/15/opinion/ school-shooters-florida-guns.html.

GREEN, ERICA L. "Trump Finds Unlikely Culprit in School Shootings: Obama Discipline Policies." *The New York Times*, 13 Mar. 2018, https://www .nytimes.com/2018/03/13/us/politics/trump-school-shootings-obama -discipline-policies.html.

HABERMAN, CLYDE. "When Columbine Is Invoked, Fears Tend to Overshadow Facts." *The New York Times*, 27 Sept. 2015, https://www.nytimes.com/ 2015/09/28/us/when-columbine-is-invoked-fears-tend-to-overshadow -facts.html.

HARTOCOLLIS, ANEMONA, AND JACEY FORTIN. "Should Teachers Carry Guns? Are Metal Detectors Helpful? What Experts Say." *The New York Times*, 22 Feb. 2018, https://www.nytimes.com/2018/02/22/us/school-safety-mass -shootings.html.

HAUSER, CHRISTINE, AND ANAHAD O'CONNOR. "Virginia Tech Shooting Leaves 33 Dead." *The New York Times*, 16 Apr. 2007, https://www.nytimes.com/ 2007/04/16/us/16cnd-shooting.html.

HEALY, JACK. "Outspoken and Precocious, Florida Students Struggle With Loss When the Cameras Turn Off." *The New York Times*, 25 Feb. 2018, https://www.nytimes.com/2018/02/25/us/florida-shooting-parkland -students.html.

HEALY, JACK. "Scared but Resilient, Stoneman Douglas Students Return to

Class." *The New York Times*, 28 Feb. 2018, https://www.nytimes
.com/2018/02/28/us/stoneman-douglas-parkland-shooting.html.

KIFNER, JOHN. "4 Kent State Students Killed by Troops." *The New York Times*,
4 May 1970, https://archive.nytimes.com/www.nytimes.com/learning/
general/onthisday/big/0504.html#article.

LEONHARDT, DAVID. "Letting American Kids Die." *The New York Times*,
17 Feb. 2018, https://www.nytimes.com/2018/02/17/opinion/sunday/letting
-american-kids-die.html.

LIMERICK, PATRICIA NELSON. "In the New West, Violence Is Real." *The New
York Times*, 24 Apr. 1999, https://www.nytimes.com/1999/04/24/opinion/
in-the-new-west-violence-is-real.html.

THE NEW YORK TIMES. "How Many More Warnings?" *The New York Times*,
11 Feb. 2008, https://www.nytimes.com/2008/02/11/opinion/11mon3.html.

THE NEW YORK TIMES. "University of Texas to Reopen Clock Tower Closed
After Suicides." *The New York Times*, 17 Nov. 1998, https://www.nytimes
.com/1998/11/17/us/university-of-texas-to-reopen-clock-tower-closed
-after-suicides.html.

THE NEW YORK TIMES. "What Congress Has Accomplished Since the Sandy
Hook Massacre." *The New York Times*, 15 Feb. 2018, https://www.nytimes
.com/interactive/2018/02/15/opinion/congress-gun-progress.html.

THE NEW YORK TIMES. "Will America Choose Its Children Over Guns?" *The
New York Times*, 20 Feb. 2018, https://www.nytimes.com/2018/02/20/
opinion/america-children-guns-shooting-florida.html.

OPPEL, RICHARD A., JR., ET AL. "Tipster's Warning to F.B.I. on Florida Shooting
Suspect: 'I Know He's Going to Explode.'" *The New York Times*, 23 Feb.
2018, https://www.nytimes.com/2018/02/23/us/fbi-tip-nikolas-cruz.html.

PATEL, JUGAL K. "After Sandy Hook, More Than 400 People Have Been Shot
in Over 200 School Shootings." *The New York Times*, 15 Feb. 2018, https://
www.nytimes.com/interactive/2018/02/15/us/school-shootings-sandy-hook
-parkland.html.

PETERS, JEREMY W. "N.R.A. Chief, Wayne LaPierre, Offers Fierce Defense of
2nd Amendment." *The New York Times*, 22 Feb. 2018, https://www.nytimes
.com/2018/02/22/us/politics/nra-chief-offers-ardent-defense-of-gun
-ownership.html.

QIU, LINDA, AND JUSTIN BANK. "Major Shootings Led to Tougher Gun Laws, but
to What End?" *The New York Times*, 23 Feb. 2018, https://www.nytimes
.com/2018/02/23/us/politics/fact-check-mass-shootings-gun-laws.html.

ROSENTHAL, SHANA. "I Interned for Senator Rubio. Now I'm Begging Him to Act on Guns." *The New York Times*, 20 Feb. 2018, https://www.nytimes.com/2018/02/20/opinion/i-interned-for-senator-rubio-now-im-begging-him-to-act-on-guns.html.

SALAM, MAYA. "Adam Lanza Threatened Sandy Hook Killings Years Earlier, Records Show." *The New York Times*, 26 Oct. 2017, https://www.nytimes.com/2017/10/26/us/adam-lanza-sandy-hook.html.

SCHLEIFSTEIN, DARCY, ET AL. "Dear National Rifle Association: We Won't Let You Win. From, Teenagers." *The New York Times*, 13 Mar. 2018, https://www.nytimes.com/2018/03/13/opinion/nra-shooting-marjory-stoneman-douglas.html.

SYMONDS, ALEXANDRIA, AND RAILLAN BROOKS. "Reporting on a Mass Shooting, Again." *The New York Times*, 16 Feb. 2018, https://www.nytimes.com/2018/02/16/insider/reporting-mass-shooting-parkland.html.

TUFEKCI, ZEYNEP. "The Virginia Shooter Wanted Fame. Let's Not Give It to Him." *The New York Times*, 27 Aug. 2015, https://www.nytimes.com/2015/08/27/opinion/the-virginia-shooter-wanted-fame-lets-not-give-it-to-him.html.

TURKEWITZ, JULIE. "Florida Students Began With Optimism. Then They Spoke to Lawmakers." *The New York Times*, 21 Feb. 2018, https://www.nytimes.com/2018/02/21/us/tallahassee-parkland-students.html.

TURKEWITZ, JULIE. " 'How Did This Happen?': Grief and Fury After Florida Shooting." *The New York Times*, 16 Feb. 2018, https://www.nytimes.com/2018/02/16/us/florida-shooting.html.

TURKEWITZ, JULIE, AND NIRAJ CHOKSHI. "Florida Shooting Survivor Wants Action: 'We're Children. You Guys Are the Adults.' " *The New York Times*, 15 Feb. 2018, https://www.nytimes.com/2018/02/15/us/david-hogg-florida-shooting.html.

YARED, CHRISTINE. "Don't Let My Classmates' Deaths Be in Vain." *The New York Times*, 18 Feb. 2018, https://www.nytimes.com/2018/02/18/opinion/florida-school-shooting-guns.html.

YEE, VIVIAN. "For Parents of Shooting Victims, a Support Network That Keeps Growing." *The New York Times*, 18 Feb. 2018, https://www.nytimes.com/2018/02/18/us/school-shooting-parents.html.

YEE, VIVIAN, AND ALAN BLINDER. "National School Walkout: Thousands Protest Against Gun Violence Across the U.S." *The New York Times*, 14 Mar. 2018, https://www.nytimes.com/2018/03/14/us/school-walkout.html.

Index